AWAY WITH WORDS

Young Writers' 16th Annual Poetry Competition

It is feeling and force of imagination that make us eloquent.

How can I not dream while writing? The blank page gives a right to dream.

Southern Verses Vol II

Edited by Aimée Vanstone

 Young**Writers**

First published in Great Britain in 2007 by:
Young Writers
Remus House
Coltsfoot Drive
Peterborough
PE2 9JX
Telephone: 01733 890066
Website: www.youngwriters.co.uk

SB ISBN 978-1 84431 265 8

Foreword

This year, the Young Writers' *Away With Words* competition proudly presents a showcase of the best poetic talent selected from thousands of up-and-coming writers nationwide.

Young Writers was established in 1991 to promote the reading and writing of poetry within schools and to the young of today. Our books nurture and inspire confidence in the ability of young writers and provide a snapshot of poems written in schools and at home by budding poets of the future.

The thought, effort, imagination and hard work put into each poem impressed us all and the task of selecting poems was a difficult but nevertheless enjoyable experience.

We hope you are as pleased as we are with the final selection and that you and your family continue to be entertained with *Away With Words Southern Verses Vol II* for many years to come.

Contents

Natalya Mykhaylyuk (14)   1

ACS Hillingdon International School, Hillingdon
Bart Bedet (14)   2
Nina Bicket (14)   3
Maren Eidal (14)   4
Luke Genovesi (15)   5
Hallie Hunt (15)   6
Tine Joli (16)   7
Naomi Kurihara (14)   8
Alex Lederman (14)   9
Brittany Long (14)   10
Perry Moore (15)   11
Anjali Seshadri (14)   12
Katie Simmons (15)   13
Yurika Takahashi (15)   14
Sam Vela (15)   15

Bellemoor Secondary School, Shirley
Andrew William Lewington (14)   16

Bentley Wood High School, Stanmore
Misbah Hussain (14)   18
Sruthi Praveen (13)   19

Bishopshalt School, Hillingdon
Shamiala Amin (18)   20
Rheanna Winter (12)   21
Reeta Sisodiya (16)   22
Shivank Kakar (12)   23
Shauna Jackson (12)   24
Martin Barker (17)   25
David Taylor (12)   26

Carterton Community College, Carterton
Ellis Spinks (13)   28
Molly Gardner (11)   29
Gareth Walton (14)   30

Tom Rhodes (13)	31
Evie Warneford (11)	32
Alicia Cooper (12)	33
Louise Eales (15)	34
Stewart Waldron (15)	35
Jonny Oswald (15)	36
Jason Watson (14)	37
Sophie England (15)	38
Charlie Harrison (11)	39
Matthew Kershaw (15)	40
Alex Le Peltier (12)	41
Tyler Biddiss (12)	42
Lauren Kershaw (13)	43
Jake Malin (14)	44
Gareth Mealins (13)	45
Daniella Hewitt (14)	46
Jamie Zoldan (12)	47
Rebecca Jenks (12)	48
Tom Batchelor (13)	49
Christie Morgan (13)	50
Holly Jones (12)	51
Brittany Daigle (13)	52
Cody Marsh (13)	53
Beth Cooper (12)	54
Alys Church (11)	55
Richard Oxlade (13)	56
Lauren Bowman (12)	57
Lucy Box (12)	58
Chelsie-Jayne Haley (11)	59
Jenni McKenna (13)	60
Holly Moscrop (11)	61
Cameron Ash (12)	62
Jamie Campbell (11)	63
Jamie Turner (12)	64
Jake Cutler (11)	65
Jack Green (11)	66
George Onoufriou (12)	67
Garry Larner (12)	68
Abigail Howells (13)	69
Aimee Wilson (12)	70
Nicola Carey (12)	71
Chelsea Paris (11)	72

Elly Scane (12)   74
Emily Evans (12)   75

d'Overbroeck's College, Oxford
Sebastian Cross (17)   76
Hannah Pack (18)   77
Alexander Cresswell (17)   78
Megan Ahern (17)   79

Downlands Community School, Hassocks
Jonathan Poncelet (13)   80
Ruby Cooper (13)   83
Robyn Turner (13)   84
Alice Langridge (12)   85
Alicia Anckorn (12)   86
Amy Jackson (13)   87
Georgina Michael (13)   88

Falmer High School, Brighton
Jaz Hill (14)   89
Luke Hibbitt-Morris (14)   90
Rosie Fuentes-Vasques (13)   91
Soshana Day (14)   92
Elizabeth Hewerdine (13)   93
Natalie Chatfield (14)   94
Charlotte Ellis (13)   95
Emma Lee (13)   96
Hannah Austin (14)   97
Graham Linn (14)   98
Sam Gutsell (13)   99
Lotte Peters (13)   100
Rebekah Harmer (13)   101
Katie Greenway (13)   102
Paris Matthews (12)   103
Katie Hoey (13)   104

Fort Hill Community School, Basingstoke
Aime Davenport (14)   105
Jamie Phillips (11)   106
Hannah Coventry (13)   107

Shannon Leighton (11)	108
Megan Train (13)	109
Kristie Pattinson (13)	110
Rachel Dearman (12)	111
Marek Wisniewski (14)	112
Kathryn Pearson (14)	113
Ben Fox (14)	114
Aaron Mason (11)	115
Sarah Stanley (12)	116
Bryony Gladwish (13)	117
Kirsty Harrison (14)	118
Tom Barfoot (14)	120
Lewis Phelps (14)	121
Ashley Jones (12)	122
Andrew Deadman (11)	123
Jenny Rixon (13)	124
Anthony Porter (13)	125
Lex Wilkinson (12)	126
Lewis Mulrennan-Cook (13)	127
Ben Carter (13)	128

Iffley Mead School, Oxford
Jake Saxton (12)	129

Lake Middle School, Sandown
Lucy Deakin (12)	130
George Flynn (13)	131
Ashley Wicks (12)	132
Ruby Perkins (13)	133
Kyomi Richards (13)	134
Sophie Norsworthy (12)	135
Cara Finnis (12)	136
Charlotte Kent (12)	137
Rhiannan Matthews (13)	138
Jake Wade (13)	139
Ashley James (13)	140
Anna-Louise Lee (13)	141
Madison Wright (13)	142
Amelia Stenning (12)	143
Gabriella Rae (12)	144
James Burke (12)	145

Oaklands RC Secondary School, Waterlooville
Roopa Baby (13)   146
Kendra Yung (14)   148

Richmond-upon-Thames College, Twickenham
Declan Lippitt (17)   149

Roedean School, Brighton
Dilly Francis (12)   150
Isabelle Regan (12)   151
Sophie Abaza (11)   152
Chidalu Ekeh (13)   153
Grace Burke (13)   154
Daisy Milner (12)   155
Eniore Majekodunmi (11)   156
Lily She-Yin (11)   157

St Vincent College, Gosport
Jasmine Woods (16)   158

Shiplake College, Shiplake
James Gifford   159

Swanmore Middle School, Ryde
Jordan Lum (12)   160
Angus Bruce (12)   161
Liam Wraxton (12)   162
Kerry Way (11)   163
Joanna Wheeler (11)   164
Patrick MacKinney (12)   165
Kiera Moore (12)   166
Alex Cooper (12)   167
Paige Finch (12)   168
Karl John Stathers (12)   169
Rebecca Horwood (12)   170
Amie Buck (12)   171
Grace Smythers (12)   172
Luke Cumberpatch (11)   173
Isaac Hudson (12)   174
Katie Bowley (11)   175

Katie Stow (12)   176
Jez Daniel Dunn (11)   177

The American Community School, Cobham
Charlotte Turton (14)   178
Morten Heggenes (14)   179
Marlaina Rich (15)   180

The Poems

After The Thunderstorm

The pavement glistens
And behind the wicket garden gate,
The garden overgrown with time,
Alights with placid drops of shine,
Its usual lilac tree resides,
Unaltered and untouched,
The droplets lie there too,
Weighing each petal down anew,
You hop on past,
You pick the branch that's fallen down,
A sweet remembrance tempts the sense,
But one of difference,
What strange undreamt,
Uncaressed thing?
Despite the comfort of earnest yearning,
A new possibly profound desire,
Attracts you past the old garden gate
And down the gilted road,
Of many vision innate.

Natalya Mykhaylyuk (14)

Dutch Silence

There was a time that I could not speak
I was really quiet and weak
Nobody could understand me
I could not speak to my friends, you see
But now, now I can talk to everyone!
I can change everyone now!
Now, I can have fun
I want to change a lot, but how?
There was a time that I could not speak
I was really quiet and weak
But now, now I can change the world.

Bart Bedet (14)
ACS Hillingdon International School, Hillingdon

Lost Memories Of Beach Nights

Sand squelching under my feet
Cold sea breeze makes me shiver
Senses assaulted:
Wind on skin,
Music blares,
The sweet taste of chocolate on my lips.
Sweet candy, sour anticipation
Perfection is tainted.

Blankets taken from the house
Huddled together.
People twirling
Blurred legs
Grinning faces
Camera long forgotten, images imprinted on my mind.
Warm blankets, cold fears
Perfection is tainted.

Scent of saltwater rushes over me.
Burying my toes in the sand
Tumbling onto blankets, exhausted.
Will we remember?
Friends hold on desperately.
Clothes that aren't mine, tears that are.
Shared hope, private despair
Perfection is tainted.

The evening is over.
What is left
So many miles away?
The smell of salt on my hair
And memories
Of tainted perfection.

Nina Bicket (14)
ACS Hillingdon International School, Hillingdon

My Special Friend

At the age of four, I got a special friend
I couldn't love him more
He was not for sharing, nor for hiding; my special little friend.

At the age of five, he had grown
His eyes were furry, his eyes were grey
And we would never leave him alone.

At the age of six, he was free
All he would ever do was flee
But his return was always a guarantee.

At the age of seven, he was a happy creature
Every day he walked his special routine
Always dragging along that black tail.

At the age of eight, he was gone
We loved our little cat so much
It was hard to say goodbye.

Maren Eidal (14)
ACS Hillingdon International School, Hillingdon

A Lone Candle

The dark is generous and it is patient
It is the dark that seeds cruelty into justice
That drips contempt into compassion
That poisons loves with seeds of doubt
The dark can be patient
For the slightest drop of rain will cause those seeds to sprout.

The rain will come
And the seeds will sprout
For the dark is the soil in which they grow
And it is the clouds above them   .
And it waits behind the star that gives them light
The dark's patience is infinite
Eventually, even stars burn out.

The dark is generous and it is patient
And it always wins
But in the heart of its strength lies weakness
One lone candle is enough to hold it back
Love is more than just a candle
But even in the deepest of night
Where the moon's glow causes blood to turn back
There are some who dream of dawn.

Luke Genovesi (15)
ACS Hillingdon International School, Hillingdon

Home

When I look around one last time
And I see that door close forever.
I've lived happily here in Europe for seven years time
Now, sadly, our time here has come to an end.
To say goodbye to people is just too hard,
So I choose simply to smile and say:
'It's been great, I've made some good memories.'
Tears start falling as I wave goodbye,
My time in Europe I will never forget,
It's so hard to say goodbye to my home.

Hallie Hunt (15)
ACS Hillingdon International School, Hillingdon

It's Going To Be OK

The door slams shut
Again, he walks away.
I see her on the floor,
Drowning in tears.
Without realising
I whisper from my corner:
'It's going to be OK.'

She stands up
Only the red colour on her face
Reminds us of what happened.
There's no telling
When he will be back.
I'm scared, but I tell myself:
'It's going to be OK.'

Nothing I can say
Can take back what he did
And he will forever
Be hated by me.
He makes us so weak
But as long as I believe
It's going to be OK.

She falls back down
More red flows from her face
It's covering the floor
My scream breaks
Her eyes search for me
And she utters her last words:
'It's going to be OK.'

Tine Joli (16)
ACS Hillingdon International School, Hillingdon

Meaning Of Life

People think at least once about the aims of their life
They wonder what they were born for.
People give it some thought
And they give some ideas to themselves
Thinking from a naught.

Some people say it is
To know happiness
Some people say or think
It is to know sadness
Some people say it is
To know loneliness in your life
Some people say it is
To improve yourself in your life.

It is up to you how you think
Although some of them are too strict and sharp
To compete like a knife
However, I think the most important thing to do
Is to make an effort
So I prefer to do things as challenging as possible in my life.

Naomi Kurihara (14)
ACS Hillingdon International School, Hillingdon

Memory

The sand is warm beneath my feet
I curl my toes and listen to the waves crash upon the shore
The moon is our only light
We tell jokes and gaze at the stars

It is nearly midnight and we have not moved
The three of four of us lay quiet under the sky
We finally get up and walk home
Matt skates barefoot downhill

My smile lasts through the night
I will never forget such a night as this
My best friends next to me, sleeping
I laugh quietly to myself, I wish I'd never left!

Alex Lederman (14)
ACS Hillingdon International School, Hillingdon

Reversed Fairy Tale

In times old there lived a dragon fearsome
So announced the king to all knights around:
(For the matter was rather bothersome)
'Complete this task and do so to be crowned.'

(The knights began to listen to this mess)
'In the cave, kill the dragon with your sword,
For it's captured the unmarried princess.
Return my daughter, as she's the reward.'

At this, one knight began to travel north
He rode off with his sword and steed and pride.
Reaching the cave, he called the dragon forth,
'But I killed the dragon!' the princess cried.

Task unfulfilled, the knight heard some laughter
And the princess was happy thereafter.

Brittany Long (14)
ACS Hillingdon International School, Hillingdon

Snow

The man in brown plodded his way down the dreary trail
A path he had trodden over one thousand times before
In three years it had not changed
And he grimaced as his scraggy beard began to collect the hail

A man in blue, with clothes of expensive design
Walked down that very same road
Taking in the white-flecked trees and bushes covered in snow
As he walked, he passed a man shivering with the cold
Without a glance and nose upturned, away down the path he strode

The man in brown, Frank he was once called
Lay shivering in the snow
Reflecting on days gone by, he allowed himself one last faint smile
As his body began to accept death's embrace
With his mind not far in tow

Through his life, no one had given him a second look
Nor half a glance
Least of all the rich man in blue
With the polished shoes and straight dress pants.

Perry Moore (15)
ACS Hillingdon International School, Hillingdon

No One Listens

I can speak. Really.
But why bother?
No one listens.

All day I work, making carpets for my master to sell
If I don't, I get beaten
I used to scream, but why bother?
No one listens.

I'm supposed to get food each day
Sometimes, we get a bit, but never enough
I've thought of protesting, but why bother?
No one listens.

Some nights, I have bad dreams
I try to remember my family, but I haven't seen them in so long
I want to cry, but why bother?
No one listens.

Before I was sold, I used to sing
Songs of happiness, songs of hope
I try to sing, but why bother?
No one listens.

I'm only twelve years old, but I've worked for so many years
A slave to a brutal master
I want people to hear my story
But who would listen?

Some day, I'll be free
No one will own me
Then, I can shout, louder than a gunshot in the desert
'I am free!'
Then, everyone will have to listen.

Anjali Seshadri (14)
ACS Hillingdon International School, Hillingdon

Hunting

Fall is full of yellows and red
Acorns fall from maple trees
All what was, is old or dead

Leaves falling to the ground
Wind is calm
Hearing not a sound
Pistol in his palm

Bears are fleeing
Done defending
Guns are seeing
Fall is ending.

Katie Simmons (15)
ACS Hillingdon International School, Hillingdon

I Would Never Forget The Precious Day

I would never forget the precious day,
The day that we met and laughed together,
I still think of you every day.

It was sunny, so we went to the bay,
We put sunscreen on, that was clever,
I would never forget that precious day.

The colour of the sky changed to grey,
But my heart did not depend on the weather,
I still think of you every day.

We stayed there long, so fun to play,
We made a sandcastle with a pink feather,
I would never forget the precious day.

I remember it as if it were yesterday,
Your touch was like rich leather,
I still think of you every day.

Last year you left and moved away,
Will we ever go to the beach together?
I would never forget the precious day,
I still think of you every day.

Yurika Takahashi (15)
ACS Hillingdon International School, Hillingdon

Why Are We Here?

We are here for a reason, that's what I say
A reason found in the nights of June and all the flowers of May.
A reason found in the dew on the grass
A reason found in memories long past.

We are here for a reason, it has to be true
The reason is found in pictures of you.
The reason is found, you have to believe
In the friendly glances on Christmas Eve.

We are here for a reason, as sure as dogs bark
The reason is a light in the dark
A bench in the park
Or the song of a lark
The reason isn't simple, it's not easy to see
It's a lesson to learn like being stung by a bee.

Next time you're out, really open your eyes
Look for the reason, it's a big surprise.
The reason is out there, I tell you it's true
It's been here longer than both me and you.

Sam Vela (15)
ACS Hillingdon International School, Hillingdon

The Meaning Of Family

Will you take my picture?
Will you take my hand?
Will you take my pain away,
That I have tried so hard to hide?

Will you watch me play in goal,
In foul or freezing weather?
Could we spend all Christmases
And holidays together?

Will you pack my lunch for me?
Sometimes take my hand?
Could we just be ordinary?
Do you understand?

When I throw a tantrum,
Will you promise not to pack?
If I learn to love you,
Will you try to love me back?

Will we see the funny side?
Laugh when times get tough?
We will be a family,
That will be enough!

Family comes together,
For always and forever,
In sickness and in health,
In poverty or in wealth,
Family to me has many meanings.

For all are full of diverse feelings,
Love and anger both within a single one,
The children who stay,
The children who run.

Can one family be better than another?
It all depends on how they love each other,
A family's love should last forever,
Bonds of love nothing can sever.

For the family I have,
I am happy and blessed
And nothing more truthful have I ever confessed.
Family has many meanings, but one rises above,
The greatest meaning of family is that of love.

Andrew William Lewington (14)
Bellemoor Secondary School, Shirley

Through The Eyes Of A Blind Person

Morning has come
But it is still dark
My best friend awakes me
By his energetic bark.

Another day has come
To pretend to be brave
But inside all I hear is my echo
In this lonely cave.

I hear people laugh
I feel them stare
Just because I don't see you
It doesn't mean I don't care.

I'm human like everyone
That you know
But by the way I am treated
I feel so low.

But some people are kind
They show me they care
Why doesn't everyone?
It just isn't fair.

I hope one day
I will see the sun and the sea
Flowers and animals
And my dog and me.

Misbah Hussain (14)
Bentley Wood High School, Stanmore

Inspiration

'To become a leader, you must first be a follower';
These words rang in my ears,
I would remember them for years.

Before I thought, I knew my brain had fought,
With my huge ego;
This saying had been embedded a long time ago
In the racing kaleidoscope of my mind;

My ego had been shattered;
It knew that it had lost its battle,
In telling me that only my opinions mattered;
I put my entire ego, in a sealed bottle
And flung it into a secluded seabed in mind.

I now know that the saying is true
Thanks to my conscience, I know if,
I did not listen to my brain,
My spirit would have been in rue.

The saying now inspired me,
Like it inspired many others before me to be,
'A follower before a leader'.

It inspires me to be,
Someone I thought I could never be;
Always true.

Sruthi Praveen (13)
Bentley Wood High School, Stanmore

Your Love

Clouds cover the moon tonight,
A dark, murky picture in sight.
The stars disappear behind it all,
As I crumble and I fall.
There is no soul within this body;
Just cold, bitter ice.
I have locked away my heart for good,
Where your love will always be found.

Dazed, I seek help from God,
But my mind casts back to your smile!
Forceful peace and my heart's silence,
Has hidden you from my sight.
I remember how it used to be,
When we shared our fears and dreams.
You are a treasured friend to me,
How can I make things right?

Feeling alone, cold and afraid,
I want to tell you how I feel,
But you don't want to hear me,
The pain for you is too much, too real.
Should I back away and build a wall
And block away how I feel?
Or should I give you a call?
We both need some time to heal.

A spiteful breeze whisks into the night,
As our friendship is torn from left to right.
How do I know what is right?
How can I calm my fears?
If I do call you again,
Would the old memories reappear?
I can't stand to be the cause of your pain,
Hurting you again breaks my heart!

Shamiala Amin (18)
Bishopshalt School, Hillingdon

The End

Every beginning,
Starts with an end.
Whether it's a book,
Or a show,
It always begins with an end.

A play on a stage,
Starts from the end,
No matter how long.
A television show,
Ends with the beginning.

The world,
Is a different matter.
No commas or full stops,
No beginning,
No end.

So, as I write the end to this poem,
I think of the beginning
And how it ended,
I think of the end
And how it began.

Rheanna Winter (12)
Bishopshalt School, Hillingdon

We Will

Life can be good and life can be cruel
But sometimes you have to stand up and get over it all
All you have to do is hope, hope for the future
Whatever your dream job, whether you're an artist or even an author

'Cause fate is all we may have left
All these stupid crimes being committed, such as rape and theft
There's no reason or any excuse
For all your wrongdoings and all your abuse

Life should be for living and giving
People should be caring and understanding
You should believe and stay strong
Be good and live long

Do good doings each and every day
Whether it's giving chocolates on a Monday
Or giving love on a Tuesday
Don't listen to others, just follow your heart
This is your life and you can make a new start

We are all different, 'same' is just a word
If we were all the same, it would be kind of awkward
Why are some people horrible, just to be seen?
But why do they have to be so mean?

My hopes and dreams are never impossible
Just be yourself and if you're ever in a bad mood
Just burn out a candle
I'm not going to change myself for anyone
They'll just have to understand
And if they can't, do you think I give a damn?

Everyone is special
Hey, we're all just people
We are all born together, we are not on our own
We will live forever and not alone.

Reeta Sisodiya (16)
Bishopshalt School, Hillingdon

If Only I Had Known

I f only I had known,
F or I would not be lying here today.

O nly how could I have known?
N o one man or woman knows the unforeseen secrets of death itself.
L ying here on my own,
Y elping before it came.

I n these last few breaths I saw my life flash before my eyes.

H aving now found the answer to the unanswerable question,
A nswering it at the doorstep of death.
D eath it came at that moment and the answer left a mystery to all
   but me.

K knowledge that no one but I possess,
N ow I have the answer and no longer it is a mystery.
O nly I know what it feels like to die.
W hen you die your soul is set free but with a burden and an upsetting
   dream,
N owhere to be seen is your family . . .

Shivank Kakar (12)
Bishopshalt School, Hillingdon

There Isn't

There is no word to describe the beauty,
No sound to match the ones I hear,
The heavenly chorus of the morning,
The feeling I have when you're near.

There isn't a motion to show you,
There isn't an eye that can see,
The love that I hold in my heart for you,
The feeling that you're holding me.

There isn't a place I could take you,
To show you how much I care.
I hope that this ring is enough, my love,
To show you I'll always be there.

Shauna Jackson (12)
Bishopshalt School, Hillingdon

When Earth Met Heaven

I met her on a Friday night
At ten past seven
I only remember because that's when Earth met Heaven
And Earth liked Heaven and Heaven liked Earth
Earth liked Heaven's purity
And Heaven, I don't know what she liked in Earth
But as she lay her hands upon it
Earth began to shake
Heaven reassured it
And Earth looked in its face
And the two worlds collided
Earth and Heaven
On a Friday night
At ten past seven.

Martin Barker (17)
Bishopshalt School, Hillingdon

World War II

Call-up papers come through the door,
Two strangers meet on the way to war.
James and Ryan are paired together,
Their friendship will never sever.

(We learn together!)

Nothing prepared them for the stench,
Or fighting in a death-ridden trench.
Bullets are whistling over their heads,
Missiles explode, the mud turns red.

(We fight together!)

A German's face appears above,
A bayonet he's about to shove.
He tried to cause the maximum harm,
But James shot him first, in the arm.

(We escape together!)

Another German with a gun,
Their one decision, they had to run.
James and Ryan ran inside a house,
Its only tenant was a mouse.

(We fight together!)

'There's nowhere to run, get upstairs!'
The enemy all came in, in pairs.
As they ran, James got shot in the leg,
Ryan turned round and saw him beg.

(We fight together!)

James tried to climb the stairs again,
Got shot in the back, he died in pain.
Ryan saw it all with tear-filled eyes,
James was dead, he said no goodbyes.

(We fight together!)

Ryan was angry, he went mad,
He shot the men he thought were so bad.
But bullet met flesh and then met bone,
Sergeant Ryan died on his own.

(We die together!)

David Taylor (12)
Bishopshalt School, Hillingdon

The Full Moon

On the night of the full moon
I have to walk home on my own
An owl squawks high and low
The trees are dark
They creak in the long, unfriendly breeze
Dogs and wolves howl in the long, silent moonlight
Stars are shining
I know I am being followed
I dare not look back into the creature's big bulging eyes
Suddenly
Left to die
Scared
Alone.

Ellis Spinks (13)
Carterton Community College, Carterton

Friends

Friends are always there for you
When you're sad and lonely too
They can make you laugh so much
All you need is their gentle touch.

They give you chocolate, sweets as well
To make you feel better when you fell
They're always there, always there to give a hug
When you've fallen down a hole you've dug.

Friends are a big thing in this world
Without them you couldn't survive
I love my friends
They are the best.

Friends are always there for you
When you're sad and lonely too
They can make you laugh so much
All you need is their gentle touch!

Molly Gardner (11)
Carterton Community College, Carterton

SATs

SATs, why do we have to do these things?
SATs, I'd rather do some other stuff!
SATs, don't forget to read the questions carefully
SATs, don't forget to write in full sentences
SATs, if you have enough time, check your work carefully
SATs, face forward!
SATs, stop talking!
SATs, if I catch you talking, I will send you out of the exam!
SATs, they're not exams!
SATs, they're pointless anyway
SATs, can't be bothered to stay
SATs, I may as well be caught one more time!
SATs, tell me why I'm in this quiet place anyway
SATs, two minutes left!
SATs, you know what I think of SATs?
  S tupid
  A nnoying
  T ests!

Gareth Walton (14)
Carterton Community College, Carterton

In Loving Memory

(This is in loving memory of Steve Irwin)

You had to go at so early an age . . .
In loving memory
'Never,' you used to say
'Never give up on the things that make you smile.'

Missing you
Our thoughts lie with your family
And those close to your heart
It is a tragedy you left us
And broke all our hearts, but . . .
You left us doing what you loved best . . .
Being with animals.

Gone, but never forgotten
Rest in peace, dear friend.

Tom Rhodes (13)
Carterton Community College, Carterton

The Magic Box

(Based on 'Magic Box' by Kit Wright)

In the box I will put . . .
A scream from Blackpool Pleasure Beach
A purr from my cute cat
And the touch of my dog's soft ears.

In the box I will put . . .
My dad singing in the shower
My mum's lovely food
And my sister straightening her hair.

In the box I will put . . .
A life forever, my new house
And me cycling
On the Great Wall of China.

My box is made from
Memories, touches, sounds and dreams
I shall ski in my box
I will see orange and pink seas in my box
I will see my grandad in Heaven
With a smile on his face.

Evie Warneford (11)
Carterton Community College, Carterton

Happiness

Happiness warms your body and fingers
In your heart is where it lingers
Outside your happiness roams free
At home it's there for all to see
Happiness is the overall start
Golden sun beaming into your heart
Happiness plays an important part
Happiness shines on everything

Happiness is like no other
Like the love for your mother
If you let it go it won't come back
If you let it go, that is that
Cherish your happiness with all your might
For happiness is the shining light!

Alicia Cooper (12)
Carterton Community College, Carterton

We Want To Help

It's so hard to know
Which face one should show
Which party one should attend
We only want to do our best
For our starving African friends
We want to help
We really do

We'll live on water and strawberries
We'll weigh ourselves on the hour
We'll wrap ourselves in seaweed
We'll bleach our teeth and hair
To show our starving African friends
How much we really care
We want to help
We really do

The party will be outrageous
With stars from lists A - Z
We'll give ourselves a pat on the back
And congratulate our charity
We want to help
We really do

We'll raise a couple of million
And everyone will know
And you, our starving African friends
Will eat again
We want to help
It's all for you!

Louise Eales (15)
Carterton Community College, Carterton

The Wolf And The Man

They run through a forest of people and trees
Across the stones and around the seas
Along the lake and across the dock
To their island once forgot.

The clatter of stones and screeching of steel
Then the winds and the reeds play their symphony
A welcome for their might and zeal
Their blue eyes glow against its fur, dull and stony.

They climb the stone cliff and up the tower
They howl at the disappearing moon
One saying good morning, the other saying goodnight
The wolf goes to sleep and the man wakes up.

Stewart Waldron (15)
Carterton Community College, Carterton

A Saturday Morning

The comforting smell of bacon
The annoying sound of Mum yelling, *'Breakfast!'*
I get myself out of bed and tuck into the bacon sarnies
Mmm, is there anything better?
The look on Dad's face is priceless
That will teach him for going for a drink on a Friday night
I scuffle down the bacon sarnies and race to the TV
Flick onto Sky Sports One, Soccer AM!
11.00am
The shower is calling as it senses the smell of body odour
And the dandruff in my hair
A good 20 minute soak will sort those out
Out I get and put on the red and white football jersey
That matches the white shorts and socks
'Come on, Dad! It's 12 o'clock! Kick off!'
Despite the hangover, Dad never misses my games
I slam the car door shut, reach over to the CD player
And put on Oasis as Dad drives me to the game
You can't beat a Saturday morning!

Jonny Oswald (15)
Carterton Community College, Carterton

Watcher Of The Water

I watch over the deep emerald sea,
I see the wild blue waves crash onto the metallic sands,
I hear the dull, deep roar.

I feel the last of the soft sunlight touch my face,
I stare at the fleeing brightness, giving way to the chasing darkness,
I say goodbye to the retreating sun.

I observe the appearing diamond stars,
I search for the ones hidden in my memory,
I slowly drift to sleep.

I wake up to the returning bright light,
I greet the climbing golden sun, I greet the emerald sea,
I get up for another day.

Jason Watson (14)
Carterton Community College, Carterton

Two Worlds

The water splashes into the dark blue lake,
Birds sing with joy as they collect twigs for nesting,
The sun reflects off the luscious green leaves and grass.

The sun reflects off the hard gold sand,
Vultures circling areas, scavenging for food,
There are cracks in the ground everywhere,
You would be lucky if you got a drop . . .

Sophie England (15)
Carterton Community College, Carterton

My Cat Treacle

Treacle has a big tummy,
It nearly touches the floor.
She doesn't stop eating,
Instead she asks for more.
You'll always find my cat
Asleep on my bed.
She never gets up
Unless she is going to be fed.
She sometimes goes into the garden
Looking for fun
But usually ends up
Lying in the sun.
She wears a pretty flower collar,
It's pink and white.
She sits on the window sill
Where the sun is so bright.
Her fur is very soft,
It's mostly black.
She purrs very loudly
When you stroke her back.

Charlie Harrison (11)
Carterton Community College, Carterton

One Day

Travelling home from the shops
On the way to my house
My house with its three small bedrooms
My house with its tiny kitchen and garden
My house with the basics
My end-terrace house

I look out of the window
And I find myself confronted
By someone else's house
Their house, with its two-acre grounds
Their house, with its seven bedrooms
Their house, with two conservatories
On the east and west wings
Their house, with no touching neighbours
Their house, with the huge, solid oak door
Their house . . . superfluous

Yet, superfluous as it is,
I cannot take my eyes from it
For the split second as we drive past
I take in as much of its beauty
As I possibly can
The neatly trimmed grounds
The accurate masonry
The sheer size of it

And I think to myself
One day . . .

Matthew Kershaw (15)
Carterton Community College, Carterton

My Dog, Kipper

My dog, Kipper, is a cool, kind canine
Who runs around every day.

He is like a pilot trying to take off in the green, luscious fields,
Chasing after the brilliant bubbles flying away into the bright blue sky.

Back at home, when he is hungry
He tends to groan and he chews his bone.

He loves that bone, that hard, chewy bone
It is always in its place by the chair
So when the fire is going, he can just lie there, all lazy-like.

Until he decides to get up and goes off to his own room
And flakes out on the sofa for hours and hours and hours.

After all, this is my dog, Kipper.

Alex Le Peltier (12)
Carterton Community College, Carterton

Chandler

My youngest brother, whose name is Chandler,
Has a life that's a little harder.
He has a wheelchair to get around,
Because he can only kneel upon the ground,
He cannot see, so he likes loud toys,
But he sometimes makes too much noise.
When he cries, it makes me sad,
But when he laughs, it makes me glad.
When our family is out and about,
Sometimes he likes to shout.
People sometimes look and stare,
But I don't think it's really fair.
Chandler makes me very happy,
But not when I have to change his nappy!
I'm glad that now when he needs a poo,
He has learnt to use the loo!

Tyler Biddiss (12)
Carterton Community College, Carterton

Your Eyes

Through your eyes I see . . .
The snaking river through the hills of misty forest
Winding a lonely course
The monstrous waterfall
Thundering out of the highlands
The sleek tiger stalking its helpless prey
The beauty of the sunset
Colours streaking across the sky
The muscular mountains
Climbing high above the swirling clouds
The city of lights and hurrying human tides
The sweeping storms of sand across the scorching desert
The forgotten temple of ruins hidden deep within the jungle
Gripped by the roots of a sacred tree
The graceful deer
Grazing in the meadow alive with flowers
The soft moon reflected in the lake
Where colourful fish swim day and night
In your eyes I see the world
Because you are the world to me.

Lauren Kershaw (13)
Carterton Community College, Carterton

Lamborghini

This is a car with gullwing doors
This is a feature you can't ignore
This car is a work of art
Unlike a supermarket's shopping cart
A car which has a top speed of 180 miles per hour
This car has a massive 600 brake horsepower
The badge on the car is a raging bull
This is the car's very famous jewel.

Jake Malin (14)
Carterton Community College, Carterton

Euro 2008 Final:
Italy V Germany - As Gianluigi Buffon

July, European Championship Final, 2008,
Italy versus Germany, two galacticos of world football,
I follow Fabio Cannavaro through the tunnel,
Genaro Gattuso behind me,
The teams are read out and the national anthems begin,
We then spread out, across the green grass,
The game kicks off and the fans give a cheer,
The Swiss stadium, packed with fear,
I stand in the posts, wearing my golden shirt,
Spit on my gloves,
Study the game.
A near chance from Totti was near,
The shot hits the bar and the Germans cheer.
Klose on the run, one on one,
Slips through my legs,
Cleared off the line.
Half-time.
We walk back on, with a substitute to come on,
Oddo on for Materatzzi,
We are hanging on,
The final whistle goes,
Extra time is added on,
Thirty minutes.
No chances at all,
Half-time goes.
We come back, told to hold them,
German defender, Philipp Lahm makes a strong challenge,
I am asked to take it, last chance to score,
Bang! Top corner of the net, winning us the Cup!

Gareth Mealins (13)
Carterton Community College, Carterton

My Holiday

M arvellous
Y ummy food

H ot and relaxing
O bjects for fun and games
L aid back sunbathing
I n the jacuzzi
D iving from the top
A lways smiling
Y ellow sandcastles.

Daniella Hewitt (14)
Carterton Community College, Carterton

Newcastle

N ever stop attacking
E mre shoots from the left
W ing
C arr misses
A ttack, attack
S t James' roar
T oon, toon, black and white arms!
L eft foot curler
E mre scores!

Jamie Zoldan (12)
Carterton Community College, Carterton

Abandoned

A udacious is a word I can never use
B rutal weather is abusive as I walk
A ustere shadows capture me
N eglectful citizens stride by
D ignity is swallowed
O utcast surrounded by vicious enemies
N ow all that is left is my fear
E verlasting danger
D rowned with sorrow and forgetfulness.

Rebecca Jenks (12)
Carterton Community College, Carterton

If The World Were Small

If the world were small
We would take more care
We wouldn't take advantage
We would be nice and share.

If the world were small
We would try our best
We would make the world
Look like Mount Everest.

If the world were small
There would be no cars
No one would be happy
Just like living on Mars.

Tom Batchelor (13)
Carterton Community College, Carterton

The Haunting

It was *dark*
Cold
Scary!
It felt like someone or . . .
Something was with me or . . .
Watching me
Somehow I ended up
In a forest
A *dark* forest
The trees looked like they had . . .
Faces, ugly faces
There was mist everywhere!
But in the mist, I swear
I saw a man just looking
At *me!*
I started to run
I tripped
And bumped my head
I woke up and it was only a bad dream . . .

Or was it?

Christie Morgan (13)
Carterton Community College, Carterton

Butchers Walk . . .

I was minding my own business
On my regular walk home
I walked past the butchers . . .
And I saw
A carving knife rising higher and higher . . .
Into the air
I heard the piercing sound of steel slicing through
Raw flesh!
That's it, over and done with, his family
Won't see him again
Poor child!
But what did he do wrong?
I got to my house . . . *thud* . . . *thud* . . . *thud*
Repetitive in my head
I had to go straight to bed
I couldn't stand it anymore
The thing I saw, I am so sure it was . . .
Cold-blooded murder!

Holly Jones (12)
Carterton Community College, Carterton

Pick 'N' Mix

When I go to the supermarket
There's a place I always go
The colours and the smells
Make me go, 'Oh, oh, oh!'
It has toffee, liquorice
And chewy strawberries
Made to make my mouth water
It is like a river forming in my mouth
So I take one dreamy strawberry
Then two
Then three
And I end up with a hundred!
I pace to the till
Beep! Beep!
Then I take the pick 'n' mix home
And eat it and it feels like an ocean in my mouth
But then . . .
I feel sick!

Brittany Daigle (13)
Carterton Community College, Carterton

Esmay

In a dark wood, far, far away
Lives a vampire called Esmay.
She lived in a castle high up the hill
And has a pet bat called Bill.

She will fly out late at night
To find a victim to give a good bite.
She flies over the village below
Spots her prey in the snow.

A young man walking home at night
Gets such a fright.
She falls from the sky to suck his blood
Then leaves his body face down in the mud.

The blood is dripping down her face
She wipes it up with a piece of black lace.
The villagers come running when they hear his cry
Esmay gets spooked and off she flies.

They find their victim, young Master Davey
This has to stop now, the woman's gone crazy.
We will go to the castle with our crosses
And we will show her we are the bosses.

The next night when the stars are bright
The villagers get ready for the fight.
They leave for the castle, crosses in hands
While Esmay is out hunting the lands.

They seal the doors with crosses and nail the windows shut
Then they go to hide in a little wooden hut.
Just before dawn, when the sun will arise
Esmay flies home to find a terrible surprise.

The castle is locked, there's no way in
The sun is rising, she will pay for her sin.

The sun starts to burn her, she begins to choke
Then she blows up, in a puff of smoke.

The villagers cheer and dance with pride,
The silly old vampire has nowhere to hide.

Cody Marsh (13)
Carterton Community College, Carterton

True Friends

True friends are always there for you,
They're always giving, but will be taking
They will always love you, no matter what we do,
They give us hugs when we are down
And sometimes they even act like a clown,
True friends always put others before themselves,
Even when they have boyfriends, we're still number one,
When we cry for help, they'll always be there
To help us get back on our feet,
They smile all the time,
They make everyone laugh
And
True friends are simply that!

Beth Cooper (12)
Carterton Community College, Carterton

Mystery

A girl walking alone in the dark,
Cold and afraid,
Why does she do it?
It's all just a mystery.

Many things that make us scream
In horror, so terrified,
Why do we do it?
It's all just a mystery.

People play in the park
On the swings, back and forth,
Why do they do it?
It's all just a mystery.

Boys act strange and all mean
Thinking they're big and strong,
Why do boys do it?
It's all just a mystery.

Girls scream at the littlest things
Like a bug or a spider,
Why do girls do it?
It's all just a mystery.

I know something you don't!
But how do I?
It's all just a mystery.

Life is full of these mysteries
And one thing is for sure,
Not many of them can be solved,
But why can't they?
It's all just . . . a mystery!

Alys Church (11)
Carterton Community College, Carterton

Trigger

Beach was in sight,
The smell of rotting carcasses filled the atmosphere,
The sound of gunshots infected the air, like a disease,
'Is there no Heaven?'
For sure there was Hell!
Four years I'd been fighting,
Four years and no breakthrough to the Nazis.
'Thirty seconds to landing!'
D-Day,
That's what men called this,
A fight with no end,
The showdown between good and evil,
'Go! Go! Go!' the boat ramp was down,
Everyone darted for the beach,
The man to my right, he got shot,
Poor kid, never lived to eighteen,
My partner was still alive,
He'd been with me four years ago, since we were being recruited,
Then dead ahead, a man stood there,
Fear in his eyes,
Evil within him,
Then he raised his evil crafted weapon,
Looked me in the eye
And before I could react,
I was shot,
My life flashed before my eyes,
I knew it, that was it for me,
Darkness took me,
It was terrible, the last thing I ever saw,
Was my partner shouting and chanting my name.

Richard Oxlade (13)
Carterton Community College, Carterton

End Of My Life

I went to a dark old house
There wasn't even a mouse
They must have been scared
We were dared

We went inside
I nearly cried
We were so surprised
I couldn't believe my eyes

I was so shocked
The door had locked
I ran through the door
And fell on the floor

I picked up the post
And saw a ghost
And that was the end
Of my life.

Lauren Bowman (12)
Carterton Community College, Carterton

Lonely Seaside

Swishing and booming, clattering and crashing,
Wispy waves against the rocks,
Like a fierce cat lurching and lashing,
The sky moody, cloudy and dark,
Everyone gone, everywhere empty,
Even the shops, as well as the park,
Neglected boats moored against the harbour wall,
Holiday homes left cold and soulless,
A lonely seagull unable to hear his partner's call,
Tomorrow morning the sun will rise,
The sea shall calm and beaches will fill,
Then this will be the town where happiness lies!

Lucy Box (12)
Carterton Community College, Carterton

My Friends!

I love my friends,
They're special to me,
Life without them,
I just couldn't see!
They're always there at any time,
When I'm sad or lonely,
Or when I'm fine!
Sometimes we laugh,
Sometimes we cry,
But we stand together,
Side by side!

Chelsie-Jayne Haley (11)
Carterton Community College, Carterton

My Family

My family is very small
It's only a family of three
There's my mum, my dad and of course, there's me!

We also have some pets
Four fish and a cat
Who, I might add, is quite fat!

My cat is called Meze
She likes to sleep all day
But not as much as she likes to play.

And these are the names of my fish
There's Shimmer, Tiddles, Will and Tigger
Who, I might add, is getting bigger and bigger!

Now this is the end of my poem
I only have one thing to say
You've heard about me and my family so go away!

Jenni McKenna (13)
Carterton Community College, Carterton

My Rabbit And Guinea Pig Poem

My guinea pig is called Leona
And my rabbit is called Falleen.
Leona is a tiny thing so cuddly and cute,
Falleen is a huge fluffy ball jumping around her hutch.
Leona is white and brown with black eyes,
Falleen is all brown and very fluffy also with black eyes.
When they get scared they huddle up together
Like they were born sisters.
Leona is one year old and Falleen is four months
And already twice the size of Leona!
Leona and Falleen, my rabbit and guinea pig.

Holly Moscrop (11)
Carterton Community College, Carterton

Rock World

Thrusting through the Earth,
A sharp rock like a Samurai sword cutting through the air
Water trickling down the rock, like the branch of a tree
The wind was like a wolf howling at the moon
I lay there in the soft summer sand
Listening to all the sounds, like the thumping roar of the lion
And I am in ecstasy.

Cameron Ash (12)
Carterton Community College, Carterton

All About Ellie

I have a dog,
Her name is Ellie,
She is always on her back,
Showing her belly!

She gets up in the morning,
Eats her food,
Turns and looks at you,
In a mood!

She plays with her toys,
All happy and cheery,
Then she runs around the garden,
Looking a bit weary!

Time for her rest,
Night-time is the best,
She climbs into her bed,
To rest her weary head!

Jamie Campbell (11)
Carterton Community College, Carterton

Winter

It was a cold winter's night
And everywhere was white
We can build a snowman
When it's light
Bells are ringing
People are singing
It must be Christmas night
Christmas lights are on
People are putting up trees
Decorations on the leaves
Mince pies cooking
Decorations and celebrations
Cries of joy
Lots of toys
Yes, I'm right
It is Christmas night!

Jamie Turner (12)
Carterton Community College, Carterton

The Day I Fell Down The Lavatory

I glared into the glistening bowl
Swirling, swishing, gurgling water
Where was it all going to?
It intrigued me to know

Splish, splash, splosh, in I fell
Gurgling, gurgling, noises everywhere
I'm drowning full of water
The force dragging me under

I've fallen down the toilet
Sliding down the tubes I go
Help! Help! Help me!
The toilet monster's having me for tea!

Cascading down the system pipes I go
Water everywhere, not even a drop to spare
Splash!
I've landed, where I don't know!

What is that really horrid smell?
Rotten cabbages, smelly feet, stinky sewers for me
Hold your nose! Oh no, poo alert!

My eyelids open, too scared to see
Am I all smelly, covered in pee?
No, it's just a dream, silly old me!
The night I fell down the lavatory!

Jake Cutler (11)
Carterton Community College, Carterton

Football

So, once I played for Billinghay,
They were my first football team.
Then, I was a striker,
So I used to like-a,
Scoring goals and getting glee.

Then, I moved to Gibraltar
And played for the Combined U9s.
I turned to right-mid,
Where I barely hid
And scored a couple of goals that were kept mine.

Then, my second season in U9s,
I was made Captain.
I scored loads of goals,
Then my coach told,
That I was Captain Marvel.

Then it was U11s,
I played with the Year 7s.
Made loads of assists
And felt I was in Heaven.

Then I moved to Carterton
And started for The Colts.
First game of the season,
I scored for a reason
And scored some more for The Colts.

Now I play for Rangers,
Hoping to score some long-rangers.
Already played in a tournament,
Broke-up like a smashed ornament
And hoping that the season will go *bonkers!*

Jack Green (11)
Carterton Community College, Carterton

The Sun

The sun
Bright and warm
Shines, blinds and erupts
Will it ever end?
The sun, nature's light

The sun
Bright and warm
Works day and night
Moves shining light
Will it ever stop?
The sun, our energy

The sun
Bright and warm
Coming, going and spinning
Our shining star
The sun, our world!

George Onoufriou (12)
Carterton Community College, Carterton

Ferrari

F antastic car and it's quick

E xtraordinary acceleration

R oar as the engine starts

R acing car capable of 255mph

A mazing power around corners

R ear wheel drive for better handling and acceleration

I talian beauty all round.

Garry Larner (12)
Carterton Community College, Carterton

Walkies!

There she is again
Staring at me through a window
Looking straight through me

Sitting in my spot
Absorbing all the sun
Like a sponge absorbing water

I run across the cold, wet, tiled floor
Looking for where they put my water
It's strange, I can't find it

I go back to where I was sitting
She's still there looking at me
Right beside her is my water

I go towards her like a tiger
Seeking its prey
I hear a jingle

I go to the door
My ears pinned up trying to find the noise
My tail wagging

It's my owner with my lead
I'll bother with that cat later
Time for walkies!

Abigail Howells (13)
Carterton Community College, Carterton

The Seaside!

Spring is here and the sea is choppy and cool
As turtles shuffle into the shore to lay their eggs
And the cold, but calm breezes,
Gently stroll down the beach.

Summer is here and the sea is warm and calm
As children paddle in the sea
And dogs run wild up and down the beach
Where parents sunbathe in the warm, luxurious sun.

Autumn is here and the sea is rough and dark
As waves crash against the shore and the sand
Wind blows against the deserted beach
As people are tucked up in their warm beds.

Winter is here and the sea is freezing and dangerous
As the waves crash wildly against the beach with great force
And the cold, winter weather brings families together
With a warm apple pie.

Aimee Wilson (12)
Carterton Community College, Carterton

Running

Running as fast as you can
The tension is on
Everyone is cheering and calling your name
People are catching up
You start to panic, you're losing your breath
Your legs feel like jelly, as if you're going to fall over
Half a mile to go, you have a really bad stitch
You stumble and almost fall over
Quarter of a mile to go, you're gasping for breath
You're nearly there, speeding up your pace
A couple more steps, there's a sigh of relief, you've won!
Everyone is cheering and clapping!
Hooray!

Nicola Carey (12)
Carterton Community College, Carterton

Chelsea's Family Haikus

Lauren
Lauren's my sister
I love her ever so much
My sister is cool

Paige
I have a sister
Her nickname is Paigeypoos
She is sweet and cute

Shannon
I have a sister
Her nickname is Pumpybum
She is three years old

My mum
My mum is the best
We act daft and are silly
I love her so much

My stepmum
My stepmum's clever
She does hard sums in her head
I love her so much

My dad
My dad loves me loads
He's the best dad in the world!
He is very kind

Phoebe
My cat's called Phoebe
She loves to fight with Joey
She sleeps on my bed

Joey
Joey is my cat
He is a playful monster
He is really cute

Pookey
Pookey is fluffy
She has such a fluffy tail
She is really soft.

Chelsea Paris (11)
Carterton Community College, Carterton

Friends

They make the world spin around
They are there to put a smile on your face
When you're down, they cheer you up
If you fall, they will be there to catch you
Friends are like air, without it you will not survive
When you're upset, your friends are there to brighten things up
Friends are there through thin and thick
Friends are like a ray of sunlight
So keep hold of your friends
Or you will be in darkness!

Elly Scane (12)
Carterton Community College, Carterton

That One Boy . . . !

I want that one boy . . .
Who doesn't mind
If I eat more than him
Who laughs at my jokes
Even when they're not funny.

I want that one boy . . .
Who likes the way I look
Even if I'm having a bad day.

I want that one boy . . .
Who doesn't mind if I'm holding his hand
Around his mates.

I want that one boy . . .
Who whispers in my ear . . .
I love you!

Emily Evans (12)
Carterton Community College, Carterton

Abstract Disgust

Teacups and flowers on merry-go-rounds,
Tragically black and red skies painting on canopies of open novella,
What does it mean to express hatred in words?
The opening of the unforgivable casket?
Or the expression of natural beauty in its crude,
Most brutal, beautiful form?
Strawberries picking leaves off the ground:
The circle of natural growth
And the fall of honey onto toast,
All aspects seem to seep into one another:
The blur of this mingled, mangled, mashed reality
Stirred up and poured into the seething cup of wretched dreams,
One cites the beauty of the trees and animals
As hope for better times and possible salvation,
Yet all of this is poisoned, infected, dying,
The water is stagnant, weakly still, overpowered by pollutants,
Greed and vice,
Trees fear fires of futures farcical, forsaken and fatal,
Trapped,
Claimed,
Raped,
Wrecked,
Washed up,
Used,
Consumed,
Beaten,
Spat on by a thousand angry fairies,
Frowns say everything in this haunted, modern age.

Sebastian Cross (17)
d'Overbroeck's College, Oxford

Formless Thoughts

Formless thoughts in my head
A clear sky on a wintry morning
Fresh slanting light makes the world seem new
Like the first morning.
Everything that could have been
Everything that never was.

Distant horizon -
Primal illumination stretching
Across the land.
A solitary bird floats on air
Soaring swift against pure blue.

My thoughts drift in space,
Whisper through sun-flecked leaves,
Sweep along half-lit roofs,
Roam out to vague hills dancing - a far off sea.

The bright warmth
Seeped with gentle ochre wash
Something buzzing in the air
Not clear but faint -
Untapped potential
All that never was.

Not the warmth of golden light
Not the laziness of the bronze sheen
Not the easy mood that lingers
Never the missing link -
But sometimes more is less.

Time passes
And still the light is morning.
The time to drift has ended.
Now I know the afternoon will never come.

Hannah Pack (18)
d'Overbroeck's College, Oxford

My City: The Angel Of Byzantium, 1204 AD

I stood on the highest tower of the imperial palace,
    Looking down as my city,
        The greatest city in the world,
            The mighty second Rome,
Burned.

Buildings I had known for an age,
    Temples I had watched over through the reigns
        Of a hundred emperors
            Streets where I had walked at the side
                Of great Constantine himself,
Dissolved into embers.

And the foreigners,
    The monstrous arsonists,
        Who had brought this on my beloved city,
            Cavorted through its sacred places,
                Staining the streets,
With the blood of my people.

I stand, watching,
    My feathers singed by the flames
        Bloody tears falling from my eyes
            And my howls of grief mingling with the people's screams,
While my city burns.

I cannot help but intervene,
    To use my power to save my charges.
        I could drive the invaders out with the light of Heaven,
            I could command them by their faith to spare my people,
                I could pronounce judgement with the voice of God,
But I have fire on my mind.

Alexander Cresswell (17)
d'Overbroeck's College, Oxford

The Water Queen

There she sits, serene on the water
So pure and white, she could be the winter's daughter.
Majestic water bird, queen of the water.

Graceful and proud,
She protects her young with a vengeance.
Sharp orange sword, large feathered shield.
Go near with care, if she attacks, beware.

Queen of the water,
The rivers and lakes are her kingdom;
The creatures of the land and sky her subjects.
She floats on the water with her cygnets.

Pure white princess,
Still on the river.
Elegant
Protective
Majestic
Swan.

Megan Ahern (17)
d'Overbroeck's College, Oxford

Poem Of The Rejected

They laugh,
They dismiss me,
They think I am not worthy of being let in on their private joke,
But it is obvious what they go on about.
I would have thought that knowing more than average
Would benefit you? Maybe it does,
But not here.
School, surrounded by people, can sometimes feel
Like the loneliest place on Earth.
Elder friends, or people recognised by sight,
Would joke as they went past.
I would reply, but underneath, underneath I was bored.
Fed up, tired and bored of all the irony, the sarcasm,
The way things went back on themselves.

And the people I had to tolerate,
Every day.
They would jeer, they would taunt,
They would persecute me for any tiny difference.
I knew more than them and they didn't like it.
So they sought to grind me down, to flatten me,
To beat me into submission,
To deplete and eradicate the threat to their credit,
But I would not give up that easily.
There were moments that kept me going, moments that were rare,
When I felt proud of myself.
I lived on these moments and strived harder to achieve,
To combat the everyday threat.

But the thing that kept me alive, most of all, was music.
I would work on my computer, fulfilling my desire,
My need for creativity, all the while listening, listening.
Music.
Not anything specific, just something to satisfy me.
It was there where I could be relaxed, where I was alone,
Where I could be myself, where I could go anywhere I wanted to.
Feeding my brain with sound, programming in my resilience,
Giving me breath and courage to face the next day.
Then, one day, I decided.

As I walked down the corridor, they jeered, taunted,
Went on as they usually did.
My temper was high, as always.
Still they jeered.
Still they taunted.
Still they struck out at every opportunity.
I had had enough.
On impulse, without thought, fuelled by anger,
In one, swift, smooth, satisfying move, I whipped my arm backwards
And swung my bag into the side of a head.
Satisfaction.
He shouted in pain, suddenly inferior.
My moment, as pure pleasure, pure revenge
Surged through my body.

But the irony,

Oh, the irony.
Again it twisted,
Again it changed,
Again life turned on me.
For at that moment, that one moment
My success was spoilt, broken, shattered.
The receptionist,
The receptionist was walking the other way,
She witnessed my moment, my revenge.

I was told by an irate woman that I had done something silly.
Something shameful.
Not a word, not one word about my tormentors.
They jeered, with renewed enthusiasm.
They laughed, they taunted, they struck me down again.
They said my Empire was crumbling.
I thought to myself, *what empire?*
A metaphor? An idea? Was that their motive?
To break my supposed empire, to rule themselves,
To suppress me, to control me?
There was no empire. Just me.
Oh, solidarity.
With anger, white hot anger coursing through every vein,
I trudged off to class.
Tears hidden inside.

Now as I listen, yet again to the music,
As I stare from a rain-streaked window,
As the sky is forever grey,
As I see the road as a blur,
As I watch the spray from a lorry thundering along,
Them,
As I see a small car, soaked in its wake,
Me,
I can already see a blue sky,
I can already see the light,
I can already feel my confidence, my resililence,
My courage welling inside me.
They laugh, they taunt, they jeer,
They fuel their fire and that fire will engulf them.
Have they broken me?
No!
Not now!
Not ever!

Jonathan Poncelet (13)
Downlands Community School, Hassocks

Alone

An impatient shiver shoots down my spine,
I scan the empty gardens,
A lonely bird flies on ahead,
A comfort perhaps to know,
To know that I'm not the only one,
The only one alone.

I stumble onwards,
Swallowed by the shadows,
Taunted by the angry branches,
Tormented by my mind,
In and out of nightmares and reality,
I stumble on alone.

I wonder if they know I'm gone,
I wonder if they even care . . .
In all the dreams,
I ever dreamt,
I never even considered
Being alone.

Ruby Cooper (13)
Downlands Community School, Hassocks

Lily

Lily is my sister,
Petite, sweet
And has tiny feet

Her eyes are like
The centre of dark pearls
Shiny, unique and unforgettable.

Her cheeks are like
Strawberries and cream
And just like a dream

Her mouth is as
Gummy as a gummy bear
And as cheeky as a monkey

Her button nose,
Plump little toes
Make me laugh

She is like a lion cub,
Cute, playful, adventurous
And makes you smile

When she coos
A little laugh breaks free
Inside of me

Chippy is her nickname
I don't know how
But it suits her

That is my sister
As soft as a
Whisper.

Robyn Turner (13)
Downlands Community School, Hassocks

Around And Around

Twirling around and around,
In a black tutu and leotard,
Dainty white ballet shoes,
Covered in grey dust,
Straight brown hair,
Scraped back into a tight bun,
So tight that her forehead pulses,
Her sequins glisten,
Like tiny stars shining in the light,
Toes as pointed as a pin,
Arms graceful and flowing,
One as straight as a ruler,
One bent and hanging downwards,
Eyes gleaming with determination,
Mouth a straight line of concentration,
Standing tall,
Twirling around and around.

Alice Langridge (12)
Downlands Community School, Hassocks

Born Too Soon . . .

Darkness
A voice
A voice through the darkness,
The thick, black darkness.
I do not see, but I hear.
Voices
Something moves
It is me, I control.
But I do not see
A hand
A hand through the darkness,
The thick, black darkness.
I do not see
I feel
Warm hands slipping through
My cold, black universe
The voice . . . so comforting.
A flicker
A blur
I see . . .

Alicia Anckorn (12)
Downlands Community School, Hassocks

Alone

Pain spirals past my eyes,
Inside my heart cries and cries,
Clutching tightly in my hand,
The memory of a lost land,
Tears of hot ice slide down my face,
In my soul, an empty space,
My emotions spin like hands on a clock,
My heart sinks like a rock.
Her smile so young, so happy, so free,
Does she know what she means to me?
Eyes that sparkled like a gem,
Was she ever safe with them?
I held her close when she was here,
Can she feel my lonely fear?
She is the one I need the most,
I wish I could see her ghost.
I want and I need her back,
So much heartbreak - I lost track.
She'll always be first in my mind,
If they didn't see an angel, they were blind.
Hate for them fills my heart,
For the days we'll be apart.
Only monsters do such things,
Don't think about the pain it brings,
I will do anything to see her again,
I'd die if it would ease my pain.

Amy Jackson (13)
Downlands Community School, Hassocks

Athletes

They perch on the block
Raring to go
A single shot
And off they bolt
The crowd's cry of approval
Fierceness on their faces
Desperate to win
Sprinting like hyenas
Nearer and nearer
They draw to the finish
With gold in mind
They pass the line.

Georgina Michael (13)
Downlands Community School, Hassocks

Manchester United

M anchester United
A re amazing
N ever out classed
C an turn any team inside out
H istory is brilliant
E xtremely quick
S uperb attack
T errific midfield
E xcellent defence
R arely lose

U nited as one
N ight or day
I ntelligent passing
T orture other teams
E asily scoring
D efeat is not in our dictionary!

Jaz Hill (14)
Falmer High School, Brighton

Chelsea Football Club

C helsea Football Club, best in the Premiership
H owever hard the teams are, we try
E very week we face a challenge
L iverpool we haven't beaten this season
S eriously badly we're playing
E very game we have to score
A nd we came second in the League

F ootball is the game
O bviously Chelsea is the name
O nly Liverpool can beat us in the Champion's League
T rying every game with no doubt
B alls flying into the back of the net
A nd sometimes in the back of our net
L osing is hard
L osing is a thing every team has to experience

C helsea and
L osing don't go!
U ndefeated champs, we are the
B est!

Luke Hibbitt-Morris (14)
Falmer High School, Brighton

There's More To Me Than What You See

My family say, of course you're cool,
I say, they don't know anything at all.
They say, we know what you're going through,
I say, they just don't have a clue.

They don't know what it's like to be me,
To go to school every day and see.
People sitting in gangs, in their own corner,
The only word they say to me is 'loner'.

At school you only see one side of me,
There's a whole other person, waiting to be free.
At home, I laugh and dance around,
At school, I make not one small sound.

At home, I have no reason to pretend,
At school, all I do is wait for the end.
I'm not myself at school, you see,
My soul just bursting to be free.

My family only know who I want to be,
When I'm at school, not being me,
At school, I'm not who I want to be,
There's another personality inside me.

School is just one side of me,
One day I'll come out, one day you'll see.

Rosie Fuentes-Vasques (13)
Falmer High School, Brighton

The World

We fulfil our dreams yet we still desire
This world's destruction never ceases to tire

We've had two world wars already,
So why are soldiers in Iraq fighting a futile war?
Earth should have amity, one war's enough
So why do we persist with any more?

What about those in Africa living isolated in poverty?
There are wealthy countries, however, they just leave them be

What about all those countries with an atomic bomb for protection?
Did no one see Japan and New Mexico go through their devastation?
All it takes is one of those bombs to go off, then there's another war,
Is it worth the death of hundreds, just for safety once more?

All the earthly disasters, like a volcanic eruption,
Tornado and a hurricane
The tsunami in Thailand led to misery and terror to the world again

The polar ice caps are melting due to partial global warming
All the violence, racist remarks and arson is just as alarming

This isn't our world, it's the world and everyone needs to care
For the effortless reason, that one day, it may not even be there!

Soshana Day (14)
Falmer High School, Brighton

But I Am Blind

Accepting my punishment every day
I sit alone in my dismay.
They say they can help me
But they won't let me be
Blind.

I walk down the street now knowing my way
Accepting me, that's the way it should stay.
I know whatever they say
It won't change the way
I am blind.

I'm getting a dog
To help find my way.
I'll take him for a jog
Every day
I'll take him to the shop
I'll know when to stop
Blind.

The television is buzzing
The girl must look stunning.
I sit with a book
Not being able to look.
I feel my way
My imagination runs away.
There's a knock at the door
I get up off the floor.
I feel for my stick
This takes the mick
But I am blind.

Elizabeth Hewerdine (13)
Falmer High School, Brighton

Alone With No Home

Every day I wonder what it's like not to cry
And how it feels to fly up in the sky,
I watch as everyone goes into the airport
And wish that just one day they would have a thought,
Then one day, a stranger said,
'Would you like this roll up bed?'
I took it with thanks,
But after that, my mind went blank,
After she had gone,
I realised why Mum always went on,
It's a shame she died,
I think that's the first time I cried
And with no dad around,
It's no wonder I found a home on the ground,
Now all there is, is me and my bags,
Not even enough money for a pack of fags,
This is the day I start to turn my life around,
No more do I want my home on the ground,
With only two GCSEs,
My future's hard to see,
But I know I have to make it,
Even if I have to fake it,
I have to do this for Mum,
But what if employers think I'm dumb?
Here I am, at the Job Centre,
Lucky for me, there's a job as a mail transfer,
I take it, it's great!
I'm going to give it my best try,
In a few weeks, I'm going to be able to fly in the sky
And now I know what it feels like not to cry!

Natalie Chatfield (14)
Falmer High School, Brighton

Just A Little Too Late

Head in her hands,
Hunched on the floor.
Heart in her throat,
He storms through the door.

Crouches beside her,
Snarls in her ear.
She turns her head to dismiss,
The stale stench of beer.

Her hair in his hands,
Her screams linger in the air.
Terror in her eyes,
But her dad doesn't care.

Her tears sting the cuts,
Blood emerges from wounds.
She's hoping and praying,
It would be over soon.

Exhausted of beating,
He slumps on the floor.
A risky temptation,
She bolts for the door.

Awoken from this,
He thunders into the hall.
He's now standing beside her,
He pushes her to the wall.

She's limp and blue,
Because of the one man she hates.
He loosens his grip from her neck,
Just a little too late.

Charlotte Ellis (13)
Falmer High School, Brighton

Suicidal Mistake

Sometimes I would sit and wonder,
In the rain and in the thunder,
If I am truly what I seem,
Or am I dead and my life's a dream?
I desire to be a musician,
Not a doctor, not a vet, not a beautician,
My friends are my life, I wish they could see,
That they are all like family to me,
I honestly didn't mean what I said,
Now every footstep that I tread,
I suffer with guilt and I'm full of regret,
Like when a gambler loses his bet,
I got angry that day
And something possessed me and made me say,
'My life is a mess and I wish I were dead!'
Now I can't believe what I've said,
Now my dreams of becoming a musician,
Can never be, as I stay in my final position,
One moment and I no longer exist,
My life is over, due to that wish.

Emma Lee (13)
Falmer High School, Brighton

The Escape To Heaven

Cold air would brush against my bruised face,
Goosebumps would cover my wounded white skin
But by then my hopes have long disappeared
But it must be my fault . . . I am a sin.
Daddy never loved me
Beatings were a normality
But never did I step out of line,
So why did I suffer this cruelty?
Love from him seemed so impossible
Like a distant dream
Hatred was normal
Or so it would seem.
So that was when I finally escaped,
Escaped my destiny
Anger just exploded in my mind
So I let myself free,
Free from those beatings and never being fed,
Free from Daddy touching me
Whilst I lay in bed,
But now I wonder if Daddy ever thinks of me
As he lays down in his bed
But now do I haunt his dreams?
Now that I am dead.

Hannah Austin (14)
Falmer High School, Brighton

Me And Also My Life

Born in Brighton
But a Scot through and through
White and red on my flag
But I'm still a true blue

Blue is my colour
And so is my team
We always score goals against Celtic
So it would seem

I enjoy my life in Brighton
Play football with my friends
The town is a good place
But I get confused by the girls' fashion trends

I play for a team
Ashmore in yellow
And my teammates
All seem to be good fellows

I like it down the marina
Where the bowlplex and cinema are too
But whenever I watch a film
I always need the loo

The food is nice
Subway is cool
And if you don't like it
You must be a fool

My school, Falmer
Is a good place to be
It's not that bad
Come and you will see

I want to be a bachelor, never have a wife
So that is me and also my life.

Graham Linn (14)
Falmer High School, Brighton

Second-Hand Smoke

I was at a party listening to a rhyme
Where everyone was having a good time
Someone pulled out a smoke
And then started a joke
And blew smoke out in my face
My heart started to race
It lingered in the air
Attacking my lungs without a care
People started to snigger
As the smoke jumped in my throat quicker and quicker
Ten years on, I'm lying in my bed
I am stone-cold dead
No one noticed me getting worse
Smoke is an unforgivable curse.

Sam Gutsell (13)
Falmer High School, Brighton

Night-Time Lie

Staring at the silvery moonlight,
Looking back on the pitch-black room,
Feeling so isolated by the night,
Wallowing in its darkened gloom,
Leering faces in my head are drawn,
Cold, echoing whispers scream
And follow me through till dawn,
Choking in a never-ending dream,
That feeling of being alone,
Just because I miss you so much,
I'm in a self-inflicted coma,
A prick of the finger with a single touch,
The red water splashes to the ground,
A fire inside me is ablaze,
The muscles in my heart start to pound,
Trapped inside this enclosed space
And the curtain of hair falls aside,
It reveals a smile and cold steel eyes,
The alive and the damned start to divide,
Sunlight pours in to show the night was a lie.

Lotte Peters (13)
Falmer High School, Brighton

Purpose

Purpose is a funny thing
No one knows what's true
Are we going in a cycle, like a ring
Or is there Heaven for men and women too?
Is there a God? Did he make Earth?
Which religion is correct?
I've been brought up with Christianity from birth
But I don't know for certain, who does it affect?
Purpose is a funny thing
I have no idea what's true
Is there an end to everything?
I really don't know, but do you?

Rebekah Harmer (13)
Falmer High School, Brighton

Unloved People

A day for the unloved,
A day for the lonely,
A day for the unwanted,
A day for you and me.

I stare at the loved ones,
I stare out of my bedroom window,
At all the people who have someone,
The people truly loved.

I wondered for a long time,
If I could be happy,
I got a call from happiness,
You came and found me.

You called and said you loved me,
You told me you have for a long time,
Always have
And always will.

A day meant for the unloved,
A day meant for the lonely,
A day meant for the unwanted,
A day not meant for me!

Katie Greenway (13)
Falmer High School, Brighton

Love

Promises said but not kept
My trust for him . . . gone
All of his words . . . cheap
My feelings for him . . . gone
Hurtful messages
Dreams have shattered

Emotions flew, but hit the end
All these kisses and flowers dead
Along with his heart
I loved him
He loved me
All over thanks to another girl
I still love him, but not as much

But now . . .

When he calls me darling
Tears grow
Drips trickle.

Paris Matthews (12)
Falmer High School, Brighton

Friends

Whenever you need them, you know that they're there,
To show their love and always care.

When times are hard and you need a friend,
You know you've got them through every bend.

They're by your side through thick and thin,
Happy to help, lose, draw or win.

Whenever you call or want a long chat,
Your friends will be there, without an eyelid bat.

Imagine if one day you woke up and they were gone,
You'd miss them so, because like stars, they shone.

So, when your friends next make you smile,
Take some time out and think for a while.

Give them a hug and thank them for everything they do,
Because without them, you wouldn't be you!

Katie Hoey (13)
Falmer High School, Brighton

I Can't Do It

I sat there trying to write a poem
But I just couldn't find the words.
I couldn't think of a subject
And my head really hurt.

I could have written about anything
From school to family and friends.
But my words wouldn't go on the paper
When would this torture end?

Then I sat back and realised
All of these words rhymed.
I never stopped to think
I was writing a poem the whole time!

Aime Davenport (14)
Fort Hill Community School, Basingstoke

My River

I am a river, rain is my source
Transportation of water
Will make its own course.
A delta will form
To make two streams from one,
Deposition of silt
Will decide where they run.
Causing erosion of all it runs past,
Weather decides if my river will last.

Jamie Phillips (11)
Fort Hill Community School, Basingstoke

Horse

I am a horse
I have a big stride
I jump big jumps
And always take pride

I like to be out
Allowed to be free
Roaming around
Just you and me

I like to be posh
When I go to shows
All glammed up
With pretty bows

I like to have treats
They're very yummy
But too many
Can give me a bad tummy!

Hannah Coventry (13)
Fort Hill Community School, Basingstoke

Colours!

Inside I am the colour blue,
Blue as the bright sky,
Blue as the deep, calm sea.

Inside I am the colour red,
Red as your blood inside,
Red as when the sunset died.

Inside I am the colour green,
Green as the grass you see,
Green as yellow and blue.

Inside I am a rainbow,
A rainbow in the sky,
I saw the rainbow when you died.

Shannon Leighton (11)
Fort Hill Community School, Basingstoke

Travelling Tide

The ship has sailed
Without me
No one left
Except for me
And my lonesome self
People on the ship
Travel with the tide
Following each other
However the tide changes
Wherever it takes them
Only I remain
Not on that ship
A crowd emerges to greet me
We stand together
Strong
Not following that tide
We stand
As individuals
Alone.

Megan Train (13)
Fort Hill Community School, Basingstoke

When I Swam With Dolphins

When I swam with dolphins, it was such fun
It was the best thing I have ever done
I saw how the dolphins came up out of the water and jumped back in
It was totally amazing
They were squeaking and playing like they do every day
It was the best part of my holiday.

Kristie Pattinson (13)
Fort Hill Community School, Basingstoke

Horse Riding

I like horse riding, it is great fun,
Putting the horse away when the lesson is done.
Working on a Saturday mucking out,
Grooming, tacking up and larking about.

I have mastered the transitions
And love entering competitions.
The fun of winning rosettes
And hanging up the hay nets.

Rachel Dearman (12)
Fort Hill Community School, Basingstoke

Football Frenzy!

The atmosphere was immense
The players were tense
The whistle signalled the start of the game
Be assured, this game will not be lame
They scored a goal
The keeper lost his soul
We got ourselves a corner
The players were sweating as if they were in a sauna
'Goal!' shouted the home fans
As they waved their hands
One all the game ended
Both teams well defended.

Marek Wisniewski (14)
Fort Hill Community School, Basingstoke

Horror Movies

I watched intently, staring at the screen
Knowing that something would make me scream
Maybe a door or drawer with a creak
Or would it be an immortal shriek?
A ghost here and there
Killing the innocent without a care
Bodies lying everywhere
And squirts of blood anywhere
The teeth pierced the skin like a knife
Drawing away all the life
I love to watch them die
In the most grizzly way.

Kathryn Pearson (14)
Fort Hill Community School, Basingstoke

The Storm

The clouds fill up the sky above
The wind starts to blow
People start to push and shove
The clouds now as dark as a crow

Rain starts to fall from the sky
Puddles start to form on the floor
The last of the light starts to die
The thunder is as loud as a slamming door

The lightning is as bright as a star
The thunder is getting longer
People run as fast as a car
The wind is getting stronger

The storm is starting to go
The rain has stopped
The sun is starting to show
The clouds have gone and the grasshoppers start to hop

This is England's strange weather!

Ben Fox (14)
Fort Hill Community School, Basingstoke

Art

Collage on the wall
Dirty paint pots on the side
I like art a lot
Paintings on the wall
Brightly coloured objects
Mosaic tiles shine
Intricate detail
Sparkling in the sunshine
Glowing very bright
Pastels and crayons
Acrylic and glass painting
Watercolours rule
Blending and mixing
All the primary colours
Red, yellow and blue.

Aaron Mason (11)
Fort Hill Community School, Basingstoke

The Streets

I'm scared and I'm lonely
More wet than hungry
Under a doorstep in a box
Trying to survive, beg and doss.

I wake up stiff from the morning cold
Tired and bruised then alert and bold
Wondering what the world holds for me
From now and next day for me to be.

I walk up the street, there I sat
In front of a shop on a rugged mat
Begging to punters who don't care what I've lost
That don't care about me and all my loss.

I wonder how Mum is? I hope she's fine
My brother, my sister and a teddy of mine
Soon this will change, hopefully
And I will come home, be wonderful and healthy.

Sarah Stanley (12)
Fort Hill Community School, Basingstoke

Homeless

Life is unfair
And life is tough
We're all so busy
But do we care enough?

Someone who's lonely
Or someone who's sad
Give them our time
Share a smile, make them glad.

It wouldn't take much
And it wouldn't take long
How could some caring
Just be so wrong?

Give them a smile
Give them a wave
Give them the care
That they all crave!

Bryony Gladwish (13)
Fort Hill Community School, Basingstoke

Childhood Magic

When you are younger, the world is not what it seems,
Your life is made of laughter, aspirations, hopes and dreams,
A simple kiss means friendship, rather than love, betrayal and a lie,
Whilst your heart can never be broken and it's trivial when you cry,
Santa was real without a doubt with his elves
And sleigh through the air,
You wrote a letter in complete faith -
Faith that the magic was always there,
Every day was an adventure, the worst thing
Would be to graze your knee,
You were extremely popular, with all your teddies
Coming around to tea,
Remember those little secrets, little hands, pretend magic spells,
No one was judged or betrayed,
Girls were convinced only boys made smells,
The world was such a perfect place of joy, beauty and fun,
Your little life had no faults, as if the world had only just begun,
Very slowly you started to grow, as did your aspirations as well,
Your forgot your childhood memories that you never again will dwell,
Equal friendship turns into cliques, comments
Like bullets they will say,
As gradually party dresses become thinner and shorter by the day,
Appearance is all that matters, you are what you look like,
Whilst teenagers with attitude strut on by,
Each and every one of them looking alike,
Being unique is shunned, as is being talented, pretty or bright,
As is having a different hair colour, or not being the right height,
The magic in life is lost, the passion has suddenly died,
Whilst Santa becomes stupid and you lose all self pride,
You lose all the memories and teddies
That once upon a time were so dear,
Whilst innocent squash and crayons turns directly
To cigarettes and beer,
Treasure your memories, live life to the full and learn,
As 60 seconds you spend upset is a minute you can't return,
Keep the magic, faith, dreams with you and never let them go,

So when reality hits you, childhood aspirations
Will strengthen and grow,
Never give in to facts, against your beliefs they declare,
Hold onto what you believe and the childish magic
Will always be there.

Kirsty Harrison (14)
Fort Hill Community School, Basingstoke

The Sound Of Terror

It was a day we will never forget . . .
The voices that were heard
The sounds of planes overhead
Then the deathly sounds of terror.
The screaming and the smoke
As people began to choke.
The Towers had been hit
Hearts ripped apart
As people began to jump
The bodies started to thump
And the smoke rose higher, thicker
And the people felt sicker
And the Towers came down.

Tom Barfoot (14)
Fort Hill Community School, Basingstoke

Junk Food

Every time I eat a sweet
I can never, ever see my feet
Because my belly is so round
I also can't even touch the ground
At lunch I want French fries
But they gave me a big sad sigh
So then I thought I could stop
Instead it was too hard so I had a strop
Then I felt like having a family feast
Which made me feel like a beast
In the end I went to bed and had a dream
That made me want some ice cream
In the morning I went on a diet
And it was too complicated so I had a mini riot!

Lewis Phelps (14)
Fort Hill Community School, Basingstoke

Feelings

Feelings, feelings, so hard to understand
Are they happy? Are they sad?
When they hang their heads in their hands
Is it tears of joy or tears of pain?
Is it shivers of cold or fright when they stand in the rain?
Is a smile fake or full of happiness?
Is a hug for comfort or for forgiveness?
Feelings, feelings, so hard to understand.

Feelings, feelings, why try to understand?
Just play along with the moment
And lend a helping hand.

Ashley Jones (12)
Fort Hill Community School, Basingstoke

My Baby Cousin

Olivia is my new cousin, she has such lovely blue eyes,
She came a little early, what a big surprise!

With a mouth full of shiny white teeth
She could almost eat a piece of beef.

Her blonde spiky hair, her pretty little dress
Oh, but when she cries it gets me in a stress!

Now it's time for crawling and clapping her hands
She could be the star in a big brass band.

That's my baby cousin Olivia
She's my favourite little girl.

Andrew Deadman (11)
Fort Hill Community School, Basingstoke

A Friend

A friend, people say is someone hard to find,
Someone who is always there, never far behind,
Or someone who stands by you, never lets you fall,
Someone you can laugh with, someone you can call,
I've heard a friend can be lots of different things,
But I don't think it matters if they don't say anything,
All I need to think about, is being a good friend to her,
I don't need to list all she does for me, when it all occurs,
Because I *know* my friend is great,
We don't need poems to help us appreciate,
All she does for me,
All I do for her,
Friends don't need to write down these things, no sir,
Because that's what makes them friends, makes them true,
All that poems can tell *them* is what *they* already knew!

Jenny Rixon (13)
Fort Hill Community School, Basingstoke

The Four Seasons

Winter starts and finishes the year,
But as everyone knows, there's always a tear.
Winter is the frost of the year and there's only one
And no one can live without the sun.

Spring is when the trees and flowers blossom,
It's when animals come out, for example, possums.
Everybody likes spring; it's when people get warm,
Then all the bees come out and start to swarm.

The four seasons go from cold to warm and back to cold,
The colours of the seasons are either dull or bold.
The four seasons go, winter, spring, summer,
Autumn and winter again,
Farmers can grow and harvest their wheat, corn and grain.

Summer is when the sun shines really, really bright
And people just love to climb an extremely great height.
Everyone loves summer because of its heat,
For most people, summer is a treat.

Autumn is the time of the year when the cold comes back,
Everybody gets ready to put their leaves in a sack.
Trees will grow and some may not, but most trees will lose leaves,
Everyone gets ready for winter again, by putting on long sleeves.

The four seasons go from cold to warm and back to cold,
The colours of the seasons are either dull or bold.
The four seasons go winter, spring, summer,
Autumn and winter again,
Farmers can grow and harvest their wheat, corn and grain.

Anthony Porter (13)
Fort Hill Community School, Basingstoke

A Poem About Patch

He's small, he's cute, he's funny
As soft as a bunny
His eyes will make you smile
His love in your heart will last a while

His name is Patch
Funny indeed
There is no other dog
We'll ever need

He runs in the garden
Very fast
I knew our friendship
Would always last

He's a little Jack Russell
White, with black spots
He's in our family
And we love him lots

But then, one day, he barked to me
'I'll last forever, you'll see'
But then, one day, he passed away
But in our hearts, he'll always stay.

Lex Wilkinson (12)
Fort Hill Community School, Basingstoke

The Blackbird

At home there are young mouths to feed,
Food is all they want and need,
So off he goes,
Dancing on his toes,
Scuttling all around,
Chasing worms in the ground,
Singing at the top of trees,
Flying where he does please,
Skipping and hopping from leaf to leaf,
Acting as if he is chief,
Making sure he is well known,
Until there is no time to roam,
Then back he goes, to his little home.

Lewis Mulrennan-Cook (13)
Fort Hill Community School, Basingstoke

Snowboarding Haikus

Smell of burning wood
The snow falling from the sky
Strapping my feet in

Jumping round to start
The excitement of the speed
What fun this can be

The air on my face
Focusing on my balance
Coming to the end

Turning to slow down
As the run comes to a close
I unstrap my feet

Turning to look back
What fun that was, I'm so proud
I go in and smile.

Ben Carter (13)
Fort Hill Community School, Basingstoke

Teachers!

Mrs Roll rolled out of her class
Mrs Clock timed her class
Mr Book booked his class
Miss Pat patted her class
Mrs Goal scored her class
Mrs Sing sang to her class
Mrs Crocodile snapped at her class
Mrs Rope tied up her class
Mrs Ruler lined up her class.

Jake Saxton (12)
Iffley Mead School, Oxford

Simply Captured By Camera

Looking through photographs,
Capturing moments in time,
Never to be repeated,
However may be tried,
Grinning little faces,
Love-filled smiles,
First tottering steps,
Tearful last goodbyes,
Remembering an event,
Speaking one thousand words,
Just plain old reminiscing,
The times of joy gone by,
Groups of happy friends,
Holding hands, grasping tight,
Saying cheese, meaningfully,
Memories for life,
Entering forgotten times,
Wishes of years gone past,
By flicking through old pictures,
Seeing old pals and gals,
Memories being replayed,
Flicking like an old film,
Discarded, unwanted thoughts,
Re-emerging,
Seeing those moments,
Simply captured by camera.

Lucy Deakin (12)
Lake Middle School, Sandown

Game Over

Life?
Fun and games
At least that's what you think
Until
Someone gets hurt

Life is like a chess game
Waiting for your opponent's move
Forever guessing the outcome
One minute you're on top
Then the next
You're surrounded

Pressure piling on
The support of your friends is dying
No one to turn to
Checkmate
You're at work
Game over
Eight or more hours of Hell
Exhaustion
Tiring
Depressing
Just when you thought you'd finished work
More comes right back at you
Life is an evil curse
Life is complicated . . .

George Flynn (13)
Lake Middle School, Sandown

Kids? Bah!

Kids?
Bah!
Yobbos and gangsters the lot of 'em!
Breaking stuff and stealing stuff!
Oh!
They get on my nerves!

Kids?
Bah!
I saw a load of chavs down the park,
Swearing and chewing gum!
Oh!
How they get on my nerves!

Kids?
Bah!
They spoil a good day out!
All on skateboards and roller skates,
Oh!
They flippin' get on my nerves!

Kids?
Bah!
But hold on, I was a kid once,
I have grandchildren and they're really quiet,
Oh!
They don't really get on my nerves.

Kids?
Oh, they're alright,
I shouldn't judge people before I know them,
Not all kids are the same,
Oh!
They're little darlings really!

Ashley Wicks (12)
Lake Middle School, Sandown

Thunder Is Like Life

Thunder is like life,
A split second of no safety,
The thrill of life on the edge,
A minute of amazement,
For wonders that lie ahead.
Ages of warmth,
From loved ones and friends,
Bright light of learning,
Education depends.
A bolt of anger,
Rage that is mighty,
But a soft glow that is left,
Love held so tightly!

Ruby Perkins (13)
Lake Middle School, Sandown

The Sleeping Bag War
(The Wolves V The Butterflies)

The wolves in their bare fur, the butterflies in their cocoons,
All marched in their packs,
Awaiting their dooms.
The battlefield was tense and all was still,
As the butterflies trembled and the wolves eyed their kill.
As they threw back their heads
And made their necks crack,
They cried a howl to call the rest of the pack.
The butterflies stood their ground, no matter how weary
And they stood face to face in the heat,
Which was searing.
The wolves, they did pounce with so much force,
That the butterflies fell with a *thud* to the floor.
A butterfly braved a takedown leap
And left a dazed wolf on the ground counting sheep.
The numbers were falling and wounds scarred their faces,
As slyly each warrior headed back to their bases.
One butterfly stood alone, vulnerable and brave,
All the pressure on her with a whole army to save.
The grounds were covered with weapons and shells,
This butterfly had won;
When it appeared, one had not fell.
She wanted to defeat, with one blow in the head,
But instead she stood straight and boldly said,
'Well done, good game.'

Kyomi Richards (13)
Lake Middle School, Sandown

Memories - My Holiday In The Alps

Glistening snow is surrounding me,
Majestic mountains take their seats of royalty,
I'm in the jaw of a shark,
Mountains shadow over me
And tower above.

Exhilaration rushes through me,
As fear wraps around my heart,
Flying through the air,
As snow rushes past,
I land and glide on the snow.

Proceeding faster and faster,
Shadowing over me,
Racing and pacing,
Waves of snow,
Looming above,
It catches me up.

Sophie Norsworthy (12)
Lake Middle School, Sandown

Scary Sounds

Frightening voices from the ground.
Night-time filled with scary sounds.
Cats' eyes glowing in the dark.
Swings creaking in the park.
Trees swaying,
Owls flying.
Cats wailing,
I'm crying.

Stars dancing
In the sky.

Moon's smiling
With winking his eye!

Cara Finnis (12)
Lake Middle School, Sandown

If . . .

If life is like a box of chocolates
Why isn't everyone nice?
If life is like a roller coaster
Why don't people pay?
If life is like a battle
Why don't people win?
If life is like a game
Why does everyone lose?

Life can be described as many things,
But life is really just fun -
Enjoy it!

Charlotte Kent (12)
Lake Middle School, Sandown

Life

Life is like a puzzle,
You have to overcome each task.
You have to think for the future
And forget about the past.

Life is like a game of poker,
You have to take a risk.
Play with what you've got
And your fate will assist.

Life is like a football match,
You have to know the game.
Your decisions in this are crucial,
One small mistake, means one big change.

Life is like a motorway,
It's unpredictable.
A pleasant drive could take a turn,
Cos if you crash, you fall.

Life is like a box of chocolates,
You don't know what you'll get.
Life is full of surprises
And surprises you should expect.

Rhiannan Matthews (13)
Lake Middle School, Sandown

What Is Life?

Life is an ocean,
It takes turns for the worse,
It can be choppy and vicious,
Like an unbreakable curse.

Life is a motorway,
Dangerous and full of surprises,
They are so unpredictable
And come in all shapes and sizes.

Life is a video game,
You can keep trying to beat that supernova,
But eventually . . .
It's gonna be, 'Game Over!'

Life is a football match,
One choice can change the game . . .
It can change losers and winners
And everyone will know your name.

Life is unique,
It is not repetitive, like rhyming,
Every day is different,
Live life to the full!

Jake Wade (13)
Lake Middle School, Sandown

Through The Eyes Of The Wind

Gliding
Swooping in all directions
Out of control
Gliding

Diving swiftly
Faster, faster
Taking everyone in its path
Faster, faster
Glaring at its unexpected prey
200mph plus

Whistling, sweetly
Calmer, calmer
Nearly stopped
Gliding to its perch
Calmer, calmer
Gone.

Ashley James (13)
Lake Middle School, Sandown

Memories

It's been a year now since you went away
I kneel down by my bed each night and pray
Pray for the days we went out together
We didn't care, any sort of weather
Just like the day we went down to the beach
All sorts of silly facts you would teach
When I got bored and walked away
You ran after me and asked me to stay.

We bought loads of sweets for our late lunch
Watching the sunset, we would just sit and munch
When it got dark, we'd walk our way back
We'd stumble along on our own secret track
To this day, I leave on the hall light
Just in case you float down and kiss me goodnight.

Anna-Louise Lee (13)
Lake Middle School, Sandown

What's The Meaning Of Life?

What's the meaning of life?
We arrive,
Stay a few years,
Then leave!

Some people waste time,
Others use it wisely,
We are all different,
So why are we all crammed
Onto this planet together?

I'll give you a clue,
One thing,
Just . . .
One reason.

Madison Wright (13)
Lake Middle School, Sandown

Seeing Through Someone Else's Eyes

You see blue sky,
          I see grey sky,
You see potential,
          I see the impossible,
You see a good side,
          I see a bad side,
You see a rainbow,
          I see a storm,
You see love,
          I see hate,

If only I could see through your eyes
Life would be so much easier.

Amelia Stenning (12)
Lake Middle School, Sandown

I Don't Have A Voice

Hello, I'm Leah
I don't have a voice
No speaking, no laughing
It's not my choice.

I feel like I'm invisible
I'm always left out
I was born with no voice
I'll never be able to shout.

I feel like an illusion
Then someone bursts my bubble
People come and bully me
And get me into trouble.

People think I'm dumb
And that I don't have a brain
I'm perfectly normal
But others say I'm a pain.

Gabriella Rae (12)
Lake Middle School, Sandown

Life

Why are we here?
What is our purpose?
What is Earth's purpose?
Why does this happen?
What is this for?
What is the purpose of
Life?

James Burke (12)
Lake Middle School, Sandown

Eyes Of Life

Just looking for a way out
Some try to learn about
This crazy life
We love and fear
Most of us drop a tear

In love with one another
At war with our own brother
Confused on what to do
Our world is becoming a zoo

In order for us to stay alive
We must strive
To protect those we love
Before they're lost up above

And when we raise our heads up high
Looking into the sky
With our last breath
We can say goodbye

To all the problems that arise
While watching the moonlit skies
Forgetting who dies
And remembering the special person's
Beautiful eyes . . .

You can delete a message
You can remove a computer file
You can erase writing
You can . . .
Rewind tape
Roll back the film
Redo the level
Or press stop
But life has no restart button
You can't take back:
The words you've spoken
You can't take back the past

Life is like a flower, opens up
In happiness
And closes up in sadness
Life is like a butterfly
Don't know when the hands of
Death capture it
Life is like the seasons:
Spring - being born to see
The beauty of the world
Summer - our hot and memorable teens
Autumn - when our days peel off from our mind
Like leaves peeling off from trees
Winter - when we budge up into a space
With a hot cup of tea and dream of our good old days

Life is like a sky
Don't know where it starts
Don't know where it ends

Life is made up of a thousand questions
Where some are beyond our imagination

But still life has a meaning and that is
'Life is beautiful if you have your heart's eyes open'.

Roopa Baby (13)
Oaklands RC Secondary School, Waterlooville

The Man That Lay Upon The Bench

Summer has past
And winter has come,
The leaves have fallen
And the sun is gone.

He lay still on the bench,
As his fists turned into a clench,
His hat on his face,
The icy wind crept upon his skin.

The wind made him turn onto his side,
Trying to find a warmer spot on the bench,
But all he found was another cold, sharp bite against his skin.

He stared at the ground in awe,
Looking at the snow, feeling an endless bore,
But he knew this was the safest place for him,
On this bench,
In this park.

Small children walked by,
They looked at him like he was death itself,
He hated it, but he couldn't really stop them
And I guess he asked for it.

As they walked past him,
They kept their distance
And some held their noses,
Scowling at him like he was dirt,
He heard them muttering while looking at him.

He never thought this day would come.

Kendra Yung (14)
Oaklands RC Secondary School, Waterlooville

Sweet Sound Of Silence

Silence sings in this night,
People stir and birds take flight,
It roars like fire and like frost,
It's the mind to life's heavy cost.

Bring us this, of an empty heart,
A sound greater than its every meaningless part,
This sound, I swear, it is such a song,
For it echoes and rings for far, far too long.

Without this, everything else will fall,
Everything from the greatest, to the small,
In that moment all is made clear,
As it erases every thought and cleanses every fear.

It will leave this world
And none shall shed even one tear.

Declan Lippitt (17)
Richmond-upon-Thames College, Twickenham

The Forgotten Green Wellies

So much depends
Upon

The forgotten green
Wellies

Outside in the
Rain

Filling up with
Water.

Dilly Francis (12)
Roedean School, Brighton

The Things I Hate And Things I Don't

I love playing with my beautiful dog, Blaze,
He can be calm, cute, cuddly and fun,
Sometimes he's fast and furious!
I love my dog Blaze, he is the best.

I hate it when people treat you like dirt,
You try to do your best, but it doesn't work,
They turn on you, then it's really unfair,
It makes me sad when people do this to me.

I love to dance, ballet's my favourite,
I also do jazz, modern, Greek and tap,
It gives me freedom and makes me happy,
I love it, though other people don't.

I hate it when people just sit around,
Watching television, playing games, I hate it,
I want to be outside in the fresh air,
Exercising and having fun is better.

I love playing sports, it's good fun and exercise,
Will I be picked? I hope so, I scan the lists,
Am I there? Yes, I am! What a relief,
Netball, hockey and rounders, here I come!

Isabelle Regan (12)
Roedean School, Brighton

I Like/I Don't Like

I like dancing and netball
But I don't like hockey and maths
I like cute furry animals
Like hamsters, guinea pigs and mice

I like swimming and rounders
But I don't like wasps and bees
I like curling up on the sofa
And splashing about in the sea

I like watching funny films
But I don't like knots in my hair
I like running, jumping and handstands
Having fun with my friends is really me.

Sophie Abaza (11)
Roedean School, Brighton

A Tragedy

Tragedies are cold and bitter;
One happened just this winter.
My uncle sadly died of cancer,
But crying just isn't the answer.

An uncle, a brother and a son;
The person I pity most is his mum,
Crying bitterly day and night;
That just doesn't feel right.

We were told at the break of New Year;
So 2007 started with a tear.
My mum was crying bitterly during our prayer;
While we were praying mercilessly to our Saviour.
Not again, I said to myself,
My favourite uncle died four years ago,
Now he's buried down, down below,
Tragedy befall me no more.

Chidalu Ekeh (13)
Roedean School, Brighton

Derbyshire

Through the trees and far away,
We've come to Derbyshire, come to play,
Watching cows and watching sheep,
You'll see their babies small and sweet.
Down the mines in the dark, stalactites and chisel marks,
Tour the village where illness struck,
It killed half the people in a month.
You can see the churches and Catherine's grave,
The stained glass window marking the plague
And through the trees and far away,
We've come to Derbyshire, come to play.

Grace Burke (13)
Roedean School, Brighton

A Dying Daisy Chain

So much depends
Upon

A dying
Daisy chain

Shaded from
The sun

Wishing for a
New life.

Daisy Milner (12)
Roedean School, Brighton

The Hat Maker

So much depends
Upon

A young hat
Maker

Sowing and
Stitching

Until the thread
Runs out.

Eniore Majekodunmi (11)
Roedean School, Brighton

An Orange Oak Leaf

So much depends
Upon

An orange
Oak leaf

Rolling onto
The road

Past a
Curious dog.

Lily She-Yin (11)
Roedean School, Brighton

Ash And Smoke

Four men do stand around a withered tree,
Guarding the symbols of the ages past.
The men that ride on in black livery,
The darkness and the fire have come at last.
No king to sit upon the marble throne,
Ruler's mind has gone, desires to kill,
Wizard's pupil faces death alone,
White they have, but black is mightier still.
The beacon's lit, but help will come too late
And in the caves below, a fire does burn,
Above the tower, the wraiths will screech and call,
Citadel guard of death and darkness learns.
The prophecy seen in innocent's eyes,
Beneath the white stones, evil will die.

Jasmine Woods (16)
St Vincent College, Gosport

Away With Words

To say you've done away with words
And still be heard, is quite absurd,

As words can be such useful things
Especially when we talk and sing.

If, say, you entered a shop or stall
Strictly forbidden to speak at all

And instead you were forced to mime;
'A dozen eggs if you don't mind.'

To silently act out, 'a table for two'
Or even worse, 'I need the loo'

Would literally be indescribably hard
In this weird-and-unwonderful game of charades.

Books would no longer keep us amused,
Telephones and letters would stop being used,

Speeches and preachers and teachers alike
Would be comic to watch (and that wouldn't be right!)

So let me make it ever so plain
Never ever mention again
'You kids should be seen and never be heard.'
For what else are we without these words?

James Gifford
Shiplake College, Shiplake

They're Just Animals

They're just animals
Alone in the woods
They're just animals
Looking for goods
They're just animals
Roaming free
They're just animals
Let them be
They're just animals
Hunting for food
They're just animals
In a good mood
They're just animals
Please don't shoot
They're just animals
Or we'll give you the boot
They're just animals
So leave them alone.

Jordan Lum (12)
Swanmore Middle School, Ryde

Say No To War

War is big, war is bad
War makes people very sad

Loved ones gone and they won't come back
Unfortunately, that's that

Limbs flying everywhere
It's like a bad dream and a huge scare

Men falling to the ground
Meanwhile bombs pound

People crying
Because of men dying

What a horrible thing!

Angus Bruce (12)
Swanmore Middle School, Ryde

Lost And Alone

I look up in the sky and down to the ground,
I wish I were somewhere, somewhere to be found,
When I am cold,
I feel like I'm old,
I've been lost for so long,
I just can't hold on.

Liam Wraxton (12)
Swanmore Middle School, Ryde

The Wedding

It's getting closer,
We're all in a panic,
It's getting closer,
We're all going manic.

The big day is planned,
It's all out of control,
It's all in hand,
We're all on patrol.

It's here, I feel sick,
It's here, I'm in love,
It's here, it's going to be great,
I'm off down the aisle, to meet my mate.

It's over, we're off,
It's over, we're away,
At last settling down,
All on our way.

It's all gone,
It happened so fast,
I'm with my loved one,
I know it will last!

Kerry Way (11)
Swanmore Middle School, Ryde

Wild Horses

I run through the meadows and the fields
I dream of other horses, wild and free,
I feel that they are tamed without me,
Always wild, never tamed,
I run fast and free,
My mane and tail whipping in the breeze
My chestnut colour can be as beautiful as the sun on good days,
Or as dark as the Devil on bad days,
Like the wind I run,
Yet quiet, my hooves touch the grass,
Like the wind, the horses run.

Joanna Wheeler (11)
Swanmore Middle School, Ryde

Poverty

People living in the street,
Selling themselves for something to eat.

It's heartbreaking to see them live this way,
Praying, hoping, day by day.

They beg for food and drink in desperation,
And suffer with dehydration.

All they know is they are all alone,
Wishing they knew they had a home.

Please help to stop poverty and save people's lives,
Because that's the only way they might stay alive!

Patrick MacKinney (12)
Swanmore Middle School, Ryde

Wild Horse

Save my soul,
I have no protection,
I've never jumped a pole,
Because I have no human connection.

Every day I avoid being shot,
Galloping the fields with my herd,
Not stopping quite a lot,
Going so fast, I feel like a flying bird.

My coat so shiny,
My sock so white,
I wish it would stay like this
All day and night.

Kiera Moore (12)
Swanmore Middle School, Ryde

Put It Back!

Time and time, how I regret,
All I want to do is forget.
It's almost a year and how I fear,
I drown my sorrows in lager and beer.
Ha! The police, they don't know,
It was me that stole it a year ago.
It was sitting there, just in sight,
I doubled back and thought I might.
But now I want to *put it back,*
Want to leave it there sitting in the sack.
It's been a burden and reminds me of my sins,
I want to throw it away into a thousand bins.
When I look, it gives me a scare,
Reminding me of a rotten pear.
That's it! I'm turning myself in,
Prison will help me forget the horrid sin.
I feel better now, it's almost a year,
And no longer do I fear.

Alex Cooper (12)
Swanmore Middle School, Ryde

Abandoned

A bandoning an animal
Is called animal cruelty
B eing cruel to an animal means that you get it taken away from you
And you get sent to jail as well
A nimal cruelty isn't
A nice thing to do
N o one likes people who are cruel
To animals
D oes it really mater if I'm being cruel to my animal?
Is what they say
O h, the poor thing, is what we say
To an abandoned animal
N ever be cruel to an animal
Or abandon it
E veryone knows the consequences for abandoning an animal
And for being cruel to it
D on't you ever let anyone, especially me, see an abandoned
Animal or see you being cruel to one.

What is the point of abandoning an animal or being cruel to it?

Paige Finch (12)
Swanmore Middle School, Ryde

Memories

Sometimes a friend
Sometimes a foe
Sometimes brings happiness
Sometimes brings woe
Some of my memories make me feel glad
But some of them make me so sad
Put them together - laughter and strife
I guess this is really what we call life?

Karl John Stathers (12)
Swanmore Middle School, Ryde

Garden Sunset

The sun has lowered in the sky,
The warmth still passes through.
Birds singing lullabies
To their babies soon to fly.

A bee taking nectar, buzzing
Butterflies fluttering around without a sound
Flowers close their eyes
To open when the sun appears.

My garden is a beautiful place,
When the sun sets in May,
The sun is going down,
Ready for night . . .

Rebecca Horwood (12)
Swanmore Middle School, Ryde

Little Girl Gone

She got taken away from them,
Only a slip of a girl.
Her mother kissed her goodnight -
Checked on her every half an hour.

When the fog in her mind lifted
It became clear,
The mother screamed out her horror

Empty in the bed - she was no longer there.

Mother and father shouted and shouted,
'Bring her back, *please!'*
Thoughts swirling in their heads, they kept thinking:
The worst has happened, the worst has happened.

Hands together, clasped as one - let's
Hope for the best . . .
Just hope for the best.

Amie Buck (12)
Swanmore Middle School, Ryde

I'm Glad

I feel bad for the deaf,
Not being able to hear,
I'm scared,
What if people were talking about you?
What if it happened to me?
But
I'm so glad,
I'm so glad I can hear my parents say goodnight,
I'm glad I can hear what people say,
I'm glad I can hear the birds fly by,
I'm glad I can hear my friends say, 'Happy birthday,'
My life is perfect.

Grace Smythers (12)
Swanmore Middle School, Ryde

Why?

Why am I left out?
Why do I never get picked for teams?
I'm not a bad person, so why?
People stand and stare!
Without a care
Why do people laugh at me?
We're all different, so why?
They don't give me time to find out who I am
Because I am new and have no friends
I just want to talk and be accepted -
They won't let me
Why?

Luke Cumberpatch (11)
Swanmore Middle School, Ryde

Dying Children

Children, children, on the curbs
Crying, crying, for their mums
No food, no food, or a drink
All they do is sit and think
Think and think of their homes
All they know is they are alone
When they're dying on the street
There is nothing they can do
Caught in a trap of poverty
How hurtful to the heart.

Isaac Hudson (12)
Swanmore Middle School, Ryde

Why?

Why, why do they bully me?
I'm just a normal kid in class,
They take my lunch money,
They take my friends,
They make me feel scared,
They laugh at me,
My stomach churns,
I don't feel ill,
But I say I do,
They take my things,
I am abused both verbally and physically,
I don't tell anyone,
I'm too scared,
I feel embarrassed,
Leave me alone, I say,
I am just the same as you,
They carry on,
I never walk alone,
Surely school is about what you learn, not what you look like!

Katie Bowley (11)
Swanmore Middle School, Ryde

Time Has Gone

Never regret
Just think to the future
Never think about the past
So always focus on the present
Because the past has gone
So relax and take one step back
Remember, *time has gone.*

Keep the good memories with you
Shut out the bad
Think of the good times and never the bad.

Look to the future
It might be better than you think.

Remember who you are and what you will become!

Katie Stow (12)
Swanmore Middle School, Ryde

Poverty

I see the proof in the street,
A simple beggar at my feet.
I ask myself, why?
Why must all these people die?
They wear nothing but rags,
Spend all their money on drugs and fags.
A poor innocent child,
With no parents, left to run wild.
Why do we leave them be?
When they cry, 'Please help me?'
Why do we let them live in strife?
When they could live a happy life.
Beat poverty for the nation,
They really need an education.
These people aren't like gnomes,
They really need good homes.
I see them lying at my feet,
Not even a crumb to eat.
That is what I have to say,
They didn't ask to live this way.

Jez Daniel Dunn (11)
Swanmore Middle School, Ryde

Bodyweight

Everywhere there are signs telling her to be thin
Judgemental eyes follow her rounded body in the hallway
Images magazines portray
One more calorie in her system is such a sin.

His arms, his legs, his stomach, his waist, they all fit into the sizes
Clothes hang off him loose as a drape
Clinging to his bones like itchy tape
To eat gives him terror - an unspeakable crisis.

Staring every day in the mirror wondering what to do
Should I eat my favourite food today?
Or should I leave it all and stay away?
Honestly, I never have a single clue.

Charlotte Turton (14)
The American Community School, Cobham

Bodies On The Beach

Dark and foam-tipped waves crash against the vessels
Filthy soldiers shaking, vomiting with fear
Odours of sweat and dirt
Taste of tobacco, vomit, sea spray

Howling wind
Gawking gulls
Barking officers
Violent, dark sea

Boat glides in
Smooth against the sand
Door slams down
Machine gun cracks

Yelling soldiers
Ricocheting rounds
Metal entering flesh
Non-stop rhythm of gunfire

Strewn bodies on the beach
Bloody, faceless heaps
Mangled limbs in the sand
A wake of blood pounding the shore

Soldiers press on
Sand in their wounds
Climbing the dunes
Clutching a rifle in their wind-beaten hands

The lucky few
Ascend the cliffs
Driven by hate
Bloody revenge in their eyes

Gun down the enemy to raise the flag
Exhausted and sorrowful, they have prevailed.

Morten Heggenes (14)
The American Community School, Cobham

Djibouti

Dark brown skin cracked from the sun's heat
Smouldering
Eyes begging for recognition as his weak limbs try to carry him
He looks at me and I feel small, though it is I who is large
He needs my help, but he cannot call out, he knows not how to.
I reach for his splintered hand and see the contrast
My white hand against his sun-beaten black one
He needs my help, but his hand slips though mine like water
He falls, I try to catch him, but I am too late
He lands, breaking into a million pieces,
Becoming the sun-baked ground
Falling through the cracks
I do not want to be too late
I do not want to see him fall
And yet, I fear he will, for he cannot speak
I must reach him first and say what needs to be said on his behalf
For he cannot speak for himself.

Marlaina Rich (15)
The American Community School, Cobham

Young Writers Information

We hope you have enjoyed reading this book - and that you will continue to enjoy it in the coming years.

If you like reading and writing poetry drop us a line, or give us a call, and we'll send you a free information pack.

Alternatively if you would like to order further copies of this book or any of our other titles, then please give us a call or log onto our website at www.youngwriters.co.uk

Young Writers Information
Remus House
Coltsfoot Drive
Peterborough
PE2 9JX

(01733) 890066